Amazing Grace
Our Littlest Hero

Ashleigh Rose Bottorff

This book was written to honor all animals, but especially the ones who have been and will be abused worldwide and to recognize all who have helped and will help and always be...

The Voice of the Animals!

AMAZING GRACE, Our Littlest Hero is dedicated to raising awareness and the importance of rescuing and spaying/neutering of animals including feral cats, while also recognizing the plight of homeless animals due to pet overpopulation that results from not spaying/neutering and the daily struggle these defenseless creatures face. Every animal lover can help and be The Voice of the Animals! A portion of our profits will go to spay/neuter programs.

Readers of *AMAZING GRACE, Our Littlest Hero* will come away entertained, educated, enlightened and anxious to rescue and raise awareness of the need for spay/neuter as well as the plight of animals due to the pet overpopulation that results from not spaying/neutering and the daily struggle these defenseless creatures face.

AMAZING GRACE, Our Littlest Hero is also a reference book for the pet owner who travels with their four-legged friends. The Pets Welcome Here chapter includes information on traveling with your four-legged friend, pet travel tips, worldwide pet friendly accommodations including hotels/motels, beaches, off-leash parks, outdoor restaurants and campgrounds. Pet services, including grooming, pet sitting, pet walking, doggie day cares, spay/neuter assistance web sites and organizations that specialize in feral cats and their colonies, how to safely rescue, and hundreds of links to animal welfare groups are also included in *AMAZING GRACE, Our Littlest Hero*, a Reference, Feel Good, Resource book for any person who loves animals.

Whether you just want to enjoy a warm animal rescue story with a happy ending, or if you are seeking knowledge on how YOU can be The Voice of the Animals! and raise awareness about the plight of homeless animals due to pet overpopulation that result from people not spaying/neutering their pet and the daily struggle these defenseless creatures face, this is a "must have" book.

Keep *AMAZING GRACE, Our Littlest Hero* on your nightstand or coffee table or take it with you when traveling with your pet for quick reference to pet friendly accommodations or relaxed reading with your pet at your side!

Ashleigh Rose Bottorff
Traverse City, Michigan

ashbottorff@gmail.com

Mission Statement

AMAZING GRACE, *Our Littlest Hero* is dedicated to raising awareness and the importance of rescuing and spaying/neutering of animals including feral cats, while also recognizing the plight of homeless animals due to pet overpopulation that results from not spaying/neutering and the daily struggle these defenseless creatures face. Every animal lover can help and be **The Voice of the Animals!** *A portion of our profits will go to spay/neuter programs.*

Please Help Control the Pet Overpopulation.
Have Your Pet Spayed or Neutered!

Foreword

Amazing Grace
Our Littlest Hero

AMAZING GRACE, *Our Littlest Hero* is dedicated to raising awareness and the importance of rescuing and spay/neuter, including feral cats, while also recognizing the plight of homeless animals due to pet overpopulation that results from not spaying/neutering the daily struggle these defenseless creatures face, and how every animal lover can help and be The Voice of the Animals! A portion of our profits will go to spay/neuter programs.

AMAZING GRACE, *Our Littlest Hero* is a compilation of animal rescue stories, all with happy endings, as well as startling statistics that emphasize the importance of spay/neuter, and the plight of homeless animals due to pet overpopulation that results from not spaying/neutering and the daily struggle these defenseless creatures face, including the urgent need for feral cats to be spayed and neutered, how to do it and care for a feral colony.

For those wanting to rescue, how to safely rescue tips are provided. Included are web sites where the reader can go to help animals with the simple click of their computer "mouse". Links are also provided to animal welfare organizations, the hundreds of spay/neuter assistance programs and organizations that specialize in feral cats and their colonies.

For pet owners who travel with their four-legged friend, there is a "pets welcome here" chapter that provides pet friendly information, including accommodations, hotels, motels, beaches, off-leash parks, outdoor restaurants, campgrounds, pet services, including grooming, pet sitting, pet walking and doggie day cares. Links to pet friendly accommodations are provided.

Benefits of the Book

This book not only has warm animal rescue stories, but the most important benefit of this book is to raise awareness of the critical need for spay/neuter and the plight of homeless animals due to pet overpopulation that results from not spaying/neutering and the daily struggle these defenseless creatures face. With startling statistics that reflect on the results of unwanted, homeless, abandoned, abused and neglected pets, this book will educate and enlighten all people, from the average pet owner, to the "backyard" breeder who may not be aware of the impact these practices have on the general pet population, and address the urgent need for spay/ neuter. Whether the reader is an average pet owner or professional such as veterinarian or shelter manager, **AMAZING GRACE,** *Our Littlest Hero* includes startling statistics on the estimated 70 million stray and feral cats in the U.S. and how the reader can "trap, spay or neuter and return"—TSNR.

Included are web sites where the reader can help animals with the simple click of their computer "mouse". Links are provided to animal welfare organizations, the hundreds of spay/neuter assistance programs and organizations that specialize in feral cats and their colonies.

Every reader of **AMAZING GRACE,** *Our Littlest Hero* will come away entertained, educated, enlightened and anxious to rescue and raise awareness of the need for spay/neuter as well as the plight of animals due to the pet overpopulation that results from not spaying/neutering and the daily struggle these defenseless creatures face.

AMAZING GRACE, *Our Littlest Hero* is also a reference book for the pet owner who travels with their four-legged friends. The "pets welcome here" chapter includes information on traveling with your four-legged friend, including an article written by the author on pet travel. Also featured are pet friendly accommodations, hotels/motels, beaches, off-leash parks, outdoor restaurants, campgrounds, pet services, including grooming, pet sitting, pet walking, doggie day cares, spay/neuter assistance web sites and organizations that specialize in feral cats and their colonies.

If you are a lifetime pet owner or a new owner or just thinking about getting a forever friend, we have Responsible Pet Ownership Tips—**If your Pet is Furry, Finned or Feathered, we have tips for you!**

Whether the reader just wants to enjoy a warm animal rescue story with a happy ending, or is seeking knowledge on how they can be **The Voice of the Animals!** and raise awareness about the plight of homeless animals due to pet overpopulation that result from people not spaying/neutering their pet and the daily struggle these defenseless creatures face, this is a "must have" book.

Please Help Control the Pet Overpopulation.
Have Your Pet Spayed or Neutered!

Contents

Part One

◆

Warm Animal
Rescue Stories

Amazing Grace

Amazing Grace, Our Littlest Hero

Dumped, Pregnant, Fighting Wild Animals and Bees

It was just another typical summer day in northwest Michigan. I was living in the woods in a real log cabin. Having been a Midwestern farmer's daughter, I grew up around animals, from the largest to the smallest. At a very young age my Dad offered to buy me a full grown quarter horse. I was a pretty small and skinny kid, but tough when it came to my love for animals. He told me I had to promise to muck out my horse's stall, even in winter. I agreed and the rest is history. One horse, two ponies, five ducks (complete with daily duck eggs), three rabbits, a number of dogs and cats, fast forward to summer 2010.

As I said, I lived in the woods on a lake. We have dirt roads called "two tracks", complete with a few hills and lots of potholes, some so big my German Shepherd could swim in—well, almost.

Early one beautiful and very cherished summer morning, I started out for my daily bike ride. As I was riding along, I spotted a Black Labrador Retriever being walked by his owner. I later found out his name was Reggie, but as usual, I don't remember the owner's name, but can name all the dogs and cats I have met in my lifetime. I approached Reggie and his owner and of course had to stop and introduce myself. (I had adopted my Black Lab from a shelter when she was only 5 weeks old. She lived to be 14 years and 4 months before going to Doggie Heaven). Reggie and I became instant bff (best friends forever). His owner told me about a "momma" kitty someone had dumped on her mom's property in my neighborhood. Momma Kitty was pregnant and had had three kittens. She was terrified and was too scared to let anyone pet her, but Reggie's owner's mother was feeding her. I asked her where her mom lived and would it be o.k. to stop and talk to her. My heart was pounding and I knew time was of the essence in getting Momma Kitty and her babies to safety.

I found the property and as I knocked on the door, I was praying the owner of the property would grant me permission to "camp out" and get Momma Kitty and her babies. Little did I know this would be a mission that lasted much longer than I originally anticipated.

I met Jean, the property owner, a kind, and compassionate woman about my age who also loved animals. She just happened to be visiting "up north", that's what my area of Michigan is called to people who come here from the southern part of my state, to vacation and get away from life in the big city. Jean and I chatted for quite a while and were hoping to catch a glimpse of Momma Kitty and any of her babies.

I received Jean's permission to come and go as necessary to rescue yet another fabulous feline. She showed me where she was seeing Momma Kitty and her babies. I was shocked but not surprised at the debris and trash where Momma Kitty had had her babies and was just trying to survive and care for her babies. There was a collapsed garage with a brick ledge still standing, which was about four feet high. In what was left of the garage, was a broken down lawnmower. Trash was scattered about and not smelling very good either, especially in the warm weather. Amongst the debris, I heard a buzzing sound, a loud buzzing sound. Oh my gosh! Hundreds of bees! And they were not happy that I, an intruder, was in the place they called home. While I am not allergic to bees and have only been stung a couple of times, I was not thrilled! But being tenacious, there was no way I was going to turn around and leave Momma Kitty and her babies behind.

As I said, this was a much cherished summer day in northwest Michigan, something us non-winter people wait for for months. The sky was a brilliant blue, the trees had just popped open and was filled with birds chirping and flowers were blooming, and of course the bees were buzzing.

I rode my bike back home, gathered up my "live" trap to get Momma Kitty and her babies. A live trap does not hurt the animal and comes in various sizes, from tiny to huge. Mine was about medium, able to accommodate a 20-pound animal. I am not the most agile person in the world. Actually, to be quite honest, I can fall over my own two feet without any obstacles in the way, but being a klutz would not stop me from my new-found mission. With the live trap in my right hand and my left hand on the handlebars, I pedaled as fast as I could up hills, around potholes, through potholes and with gravel flying and dirt blowing in my face. I traveled to the scene where Momma Kitty was raising her babies. This would be a part of my daily life for three, four and sometimes five times a day for quite some time.

Having a bike with hand brakes and the trap swaying and swinging against the wind in my right hand, I steered with my left. With great difficulty, while going up hills, I pedaled fast and while going down hills, I dragged my feet to slow down.

I made it! I had arrived at the dilapidated garage complete with trash and hundreds of bees. I tried to explain to the bees I was harmless and only wanted the kitties. I don't think I got through to them, but they seemed to understand, I guess in bee language that I was a good human. And yes, I do talk to animals! I climbed through the trash and onto the top of the lawnmower engine that was teetering amongst the trash. The lawnmower was not stable and neither was my footing. And it was actually very hot. So with apprehension and determination, I managed to lift the trap onto the brick ledge that seemed fairly stable, with only a few missing bricks. I opened the trap, bid the bees a good afternoon and headed for home for more necessary supplies.

Realizing the bees would not always welcome me as they had on this first visit, I knew it was best to protect myself as best I could without completely suiting up in a bee keeper's outfit. I put on long sleeves, long pants, heavy knee socks, a winter stocking hat and my winter coat for additional protection from the new found bbff (best bee friends forever).

Like I said, I wait for months for spring and summer, and love 80 degree weather but bundling up like I did for yet another blizzard in our harsh winters in the middle of summer was a bit much even for me. I was however, grateful it was summer and not winter because Momma Kitty and her babies would not have survived.

Grabbing a tote bag, I "fished" in my pantry for whatever smelly food I had. With cans of tuna in hand along with a can opener, plastic bowls for water, and small pitcher of water, I bravely got back on my bike to continue my mission. I am sure I looked strange to my neighbors, whom I had known for almost 20 years. However, they probably just thought, "There's goes Ashleigh. I wonder what critter she'll bring home today?" A couple of cars drove past me with questioning glances but with a smile and a quick nod I pedaled and pedaled and pedaled.

Making the trip to Momma Kitty's home this time was not nearly as challenging as with the live trap in tow. I tied a tote bag to the handlebars, so I had two free hands with which to brake and steer. As I approached the collapsed garage, the bees were buzzing and taking very serious note of me as if to say "You're back. You are either very brave or very stupid". I thought probably a lot of both.

But I was determined. I sat on the engine of the lawn mower, the only place I could sit except in the pile of trash. I pulled down my stocking cap that left only the slits of my eyes showing. I opened the tuna and very carefully, I put it in the rear of the trap. I then set the trap. The way this particular trap works is to put food in the rear so the animal has to walk across the front part that is pulled up elevated just enough to allow an animal entrance. The weight of the animal will drop the door and the animal will then be inside the trap. I sat for a long time waiting for any sign of Momma Kitty.

Belle

I heard a little tiny rustle in the surrounding woods. As we have wildlife in our woods, I was not sure what I was attracting with the tuna. With the strong smell and the wind blowing, any animal from a bear to a raccoon to an opossum or just a little gray squirrel could be my visitor coming for some lunch. I very stealthily got up off the lawn mower to get a better view. Facing the four foot brick wall did not allow me a clear view into the woods. I went around the corner and to my total amazement and with a suppressed gasp, I saw these two huge emerald green eyes peering back at me from about ten feet away. Whispering and holding in my excitement, I started talking to Momma Kitty in the most gentle, yet quivering voice I could muster.

Stunned, startled and still very much afraid, she just stared at me. I then opened another can of tuna and threw her little pieces. She pounced on them like a starving kitty, which she was. Still there was no sign of her babies. I continued tossing little morsels of tuna her way for about an hour. I did not want to completely fill her tummy, as I wanted her to go into the trap for more tuna.

She then scampered away. I pedaled back home, leaving the tuna in the set trap. And the bees bid me farewell. They did not know I'd be back in the morning.

The next morning, bright and early, I suited up again, pedaled hard and fast with more tuna, can opener and fresh water to Momma Kitty's home. Again, I found my favorite seat, on top of the lawn mower engine, with bees buzzing. The look in their beady little bee eyes this time was one of "I can't believe she's back!" This time I heard the tiny rustle again; only it was sooner than I anticipated. I sneaked around the corner of the brick wall and there she was – Momma Kitty, with those huge emerald green eyes, peering at me, still unsure of what to do. I opened another can of tuna, threw her some more pieces and then took my seat again. I was about three feet from the brick wall where the live trap sat, waiting for Momma Kitty.

This routine was repeated for several days, several times a day, sometimes three, four or five times. I was developing a trust with Momma Kitty. I wanted her to know I was a good human.

About a week after recreating this scene many times, as I was sitting on the lawn mower engine, Momma Kitty came to the live trap. She was so tiny and frail. She could not have weighed more than five or six pounds. As I held my breath, only four feet from her and the trap, with bees buzzing, she went into the trap. I was waiting for the trap to spring close behind her, but that did not happen!

She didn't weigh enough! Oh my gosh! Now what? She ate the tuna and retreated back into the woods.

We have a music camp and boarding school nearby, only about a mile up the road from Momma Kitty's home. I pedaled back home and changed into summer clothes and then proceeded to go to the maintenance garage of the school. I thought they would have live traps as they try to relocate the wildlife such as raccoons and opossums from outside the school's dormitories. I knew the supervisor and of course he remembered helping me with a rescue a few years before. They showed me the various traps and I chose the tiniest one they had.

With the trap in my right hand and my left hand on the handlebars, I pedaled and pedaled and pedaled back to Momma Kitty's home. I dropped off the trap, went back home and suited up again to visit my new found bbff (best bee friends forever). I gathered more tuna and a can opener and fresh water for Momma Kitty and her babies.

Resuming my seat on the lawn mower engine after a brief intermission, I heard the tiny rustle in the woods. I knew that each time I was there, the rustle was coming sooner than the times before. I knew Momma Kitty was starting to trust me.

Again, I threw her some tuna, but not as much as before. I then put tuna inside the trap, set the trap and waited for her to jump up onto the brick ledge and go into the trap. This time, she not only made it into the trap, she ate the tuna and when attempting to get out of the trap, it sprung! But somehow, being so tiny, she was able to get out just in the nick of time. She ran into the woods!

I went home and cried, thinking she was already so traumatized from being dumped in the woods and having her babies alone. Now she was more scared from the trap. I thought I would never get her. I prayed for help and guidance and told her, in my mind, I will never give up on you Momma Kitty!

I returned to her home, several times and for several days. It was different now. I thought I had lost her trust completely and forever. But this time, I saw one of her babies, a teeny, tiny, kitten, barely a month old, and not weighing more than two pounds. He had the same big green eyes and lots of gray and white fur. If it had not been for the eyes, I would have guessed this was just fur and not a real kitten.

I continued throwing tuna for Momma Kitty and now for one of her three babies. This continued for several days and several times a day. The trap was always set with fresh tuna, but nothing was in the trap when I checked it. . .until. . .

One morning, Jean, the owner of the property, called me and said "There is something in your trap". I was so ecstatic, I could not "suit up" fast enough. Pedaling as fast and hard as I could, I came up to the hill and almost crashed going down it to see which kitten I had trapped.

I flew off my bike, not even putting down the kickstand. Around the corner I charged and to my total amazement, it was not a kitten! It was, as I have named all the wildlife, Mr. O. Possum! He was very claustrophobic and had clawed the bottom of the trap. It being a heavy gauge wire, there was grass and dirt everywhere and the poor opossum, was clearly not a happy critter.

I noticed his extremely long claws and very quietly told him "It must take you a long time to do your nails". I was trying desperately to calm him down (and myself). He was truly a magnificent creature and to be so close to him was not only an honor but also very nerve wracking. I knew I had to release the trap and to do so, I needed to put my hands on the door of the trap and open it for him to get out! I don't know who wanted which more, him to get out or for me to get him out. We were both scared.

I love animals and respect them, domestic or wild and I am always careful when working with them. This was a wild creature that had gotten himself into a predicament. It was my job and responsibility to get him out of it. I wanted both of us to be safe. I talked to him in a very soothing voice, although I was very scared. I know he sensed it, but I tried to convince him I was a good human. He started to calm down, so I very carefully and methodically started to open the door. It took both hands. I made sure I was on as stable land as I could find amongst the debris I was standing on. I pointed the opening of the trap towards the woods. I told him "Now when I open the door, you're going to go that way—(pointing to the woods)!" I slowly opened the door and before I could blink my eyes, Mr. O. Possum was headed for the woods. I never laid eyes on that particular opossum again.

After getting myself calm again, although I appeared calm on the outside, on the inside my heart was pounding, I took a deep breath and set the trap again, complete with tuna. Again, I heard the tiny rustle, but this time, I heard two tiny rustle sounds, Momma Kitty and her little gray fur ball. I threw tuna to them and resumed my seat on the lawn mower engine. To my total amazement, the tiny, gray, fur ball jumped on the brick ledge and approached the trap. I was thinking he is not as scared as his Momma and maybe he'll go in the trap. I was ready this time! I did not want him to get out as Momma Kitty had done. In the trap he went and started eating tuna. His weight did not set the trap closed, so I slowly got up, with as little motion as possible and set the trap myself.

The little fur ball was scared and started jumping and bolting against the sides of the trap. I spoke soothingly to him and eventually he calmed down. I took the trap off the ledge, held it in my right hand and with my left hand steered my bike home.

When I got home, I knew I had to close the windows because although I had screens, if an animal is stressed enough, no matter how tiny, they will try to go through the screens. I set the trap on the floor in my kitchen. I gave fur ball some time to adjust and about an hour later, I opened the trap, fed him some tuna, showed him where the water bowl was and took the trap back to Momma Kitty's home.

Throwing tuna, talking to Momma Kitty, I began to sing to her. I did not know if that was a good idea or a bad idea, but I was tired of listening to myself just talk. With those emerald eyes, she made her appearance, ate some tuna and jumped on the ledge faster than before. I was thankful because I was so afraid she would never get near me or the trap after the last fiasco of her getting in the trap, only to bolt out the door, as it was springing closed.

Again, she didn't set the trap to close, but I knew she still trusted me. I continued feeding her tuna and praying she would get in the trap long enough for me to set it.

I talked to the property owner who assured me Momma Kitty had a total of three kittens. One was fur ball who was safely in my home now. One of the other kittens was a little cream colored kitten with aqua blue eyes. Her third kitten was gray and white.

I kept a vigilant look out for them as I had not seen either of these two kittens. Finally, after about three weeks, I heard Momma Kitty and a lot of rustles this time coming in for breakfast. There they were, her other two little babies. I was surprised they were alive, considering their size and how long they had been living in the wild.

Days later, I eventually live trapped the cream colored kitten. It was extremely difficult taking her home as she was the most claustrophobic of the bunch and I was certain I was going to crash on my bike with her in the trap, but by the grace of God I kept my composure and balance and all was well.

The last kitten to be rescued was a short-hair, gray and white kitten who had only one eye. She was the calmest of the bunch and I easily live trapped her and took her home.

Momma kitty was a different story. I knew I had a challenge here. I was running out of chances to get her. I spoke to the property owner again and she told me Momma Kitty was acting very depressed especially since her babies were "gone". Now I was afraid for her not just physically but mentally. Animals can actually give up but I knew I would never give up on Momma Kitty.

She was getting used to being "hand fed" by me each time I threw her tuna. This was not good. I really needed to live trap her and get her home. I decided to fry up some fresh white fish. I put her little gray fur ball and steaming white fish along with an old shoestring into my pet carrier. With my carrier in my right hand, while steering and braking with my left, I pedaled back to Momma Kitty's home. I carefully took fur ball out of the carrier. As he was relatively calm, especially considering his introduction into the world, I was not worried he would jump out of my arms. I took the shoestring, tied it around his little neck and tied it to the inside of the trap. I then put the still steaming white fish into the trap, sat down on the engine of the lawnmower and prayed Momma Kitty would come by for lunch soon.

MeMe

Hearing the tiny rustle, I held my breath. She jumped onto the brick ledge. When she saw her fur ball, I really and truly know she smiled. She quickly went into the trap, started eating the white fish while grooming her baby. I closed the trap and with the trap in my right hand and steering and braking with my left hand, I pedaled for home. Momma Kitty really challenged my balancing skills or I should say the lack of them as she was very upset and jerked from side to side in the trap. We made it home in one piece!

I let her and her baby calm down and released them both into their new home. She immediately bolted towards the windows (which were still closed) but stopped before hitting it. She hid for several days, but I knew she was safe.

It's been almost three years since that beautiful day in summer that a simple bike ride resulted in making four new fabulous feline friends—Momma Kitty is now Amazing Grace (named Amazing Grace because without the grace of God, I never would have been able to rescue her), "fur ball" is MeMe (part Maine coon—meaning very fluffy, with little tufts of fur in his ears), the one-eyed kitten is named Maggie, and the beautiful cream colored kitten with the aqua blue eyes is Belle Jewell (also part Siamese). They of course were immediately spayed or neutered and Grace's babies are now bigger than she is.

For two and a half years, she was terrified of men and would run at the sight or sound of them. Then one day, a friend of mine came over and started petting her. Amazingly, she let him pet her and even hold her!

Miracles do happen—as they did with *AMAZING GRACE, Our Littlest Hero*, MeMe, Maggie and Belle on that summer day in 2010. The one who actually rescued Grace

Maggie

is Reggie, the beautiful Black Labrador Retriever, whom without having made his acquaintance, I would never have known about Grace and her little family.

P.S. And yes, in case you're wondering, I sing "Amazing Grace" to *AMAZING GRACE, Our Littlest Hero*.

Amazing Grace

Sir Goldie Gandhi van Gogh

Sir Goldie Gandhi van Gogh

Starving, shot and smelling like a skunk,
who loved to "head butt"!

As I was working in my yard on a beautiful spring day, I felt like something was watching me. As I turned around, there was a full-grown cat, a longhaired Torti. He was sitting on a neighbor's steps. My neighbors were out of town and as I knew all of my neighbors and the critters in the neighborhood, this was a new kitty, probably dumped as so many were. I slowly approached kitty and he was scared and traumatized. I could not get within five feet of him or he would run under the deck. I went and got some tuna and set it on the steps for him. I have found that one of the best ways to make friends with a critter is to offer them food. I went back to my yard and watched. He slowly and with much apprehension, approached the can of tuna and before I could blink my eyes, he was devouring the food. He was clearly starving and looked dehydrated too. I brought him a bowl of water and this time some cat food and left it on the steps.

I knew I would not be able to just pick him up and take him home. I got my live trap, placed more food and water in it and went inside. Even though he was hungry, he approached the trap but would not go in to get the food.

It was getting dark, so I stopped watching the trap, but listened and within just a few minutes, I heard the trap spring. I ran outside and there he was in the trap. I brought it in my home and placed it on the kitchen floor. I knew this was another fabulous feline, but he could have been a skunk. My other pets surrounded the trap, sniffing, some running into the other rooms, some looking at me as if to say "why did you bring a skunk home"?

I gave kitty more food and water and he spent the night in the trap. He was still very scared and the last thing he needed was to get a bath, although he desperately needed one.

The next morning, he appeared a lot calmer, I fed him some more and slowly opened the trap. He actually started to come out to greet his new friends, but quickly retreated back into the trap. Waiting patiently with my kitchen smelling more like a skunk than ever, I slowly coaxed kitty to come out of the trap. I talked soothingly and calmly to him telling him we were not going to hurt him. I already had my kitty bath supplies ready, bath towel, shampoo, sponge and cup for dipping water onto kitty.

Kitty seemed to know all would be well and he let me not only pick him up, but he let me bathe him. I went through a half of bottle of shampoo and even more conditioner. He was smelling a lot better. So was my kitchen.

As I got a good look at kitty, I noticed he had one ear that was gone. It had been torn off, probably in a fight. As I was trying to come up with a name, I saw how that although he was a very large kitty, he had made no signs of aggression to me or the other pets. I had recently had another kitty, "Goldie" go to Kitty Heaven, so this new kitty now had his name—Sir Goldie Gandhi (because he was so gentle) van Gogh (because of him missing one ear).

After his bath, Sir Goldie Gandhi van Gogh let me hold him wrapped in the towel, much like we do our newborn babies. Smelling better, relaxing and becoming more beautiful, I noticed he was very long haired and not only did he like to be held, as I was examining his one missing ear, he gently nudged my head with his head. He gave me a "head butt".

So on that day, Sir Goldie Gandhi van Gogh who loved to "head butt" was now in his forever home.

I took him to my veterinarian for an exam and not only was Goldie wanting to "head butt" the vet (and she responded appropriately and "head butted" him back), she also discovered he had been shot with a pellet gun. She removed the pellet and also told me that it was true, he lost an ear in a cat fight and had clearly had a rough life. But that rough life ended that day when I was working in my yard and felt something watching me. I thanked God for yet another addition to my critter family.

A Missouri Snapping Turtle

Crossing the interstate
complete with a concrete barrier

I was traveling through Missouri one summer and of course with my two dogs, my Black Labrador Retriever, Ellie Rose and my German Shepherd Rosie. As we were driving down the 4 lane interstate, complete with concrete barrier in the middle, I noticed something huge in the road. I knew it was not a deer because it was not tall enough and yet it was too big and round to be dog or cat. I slowed down and looked over and to my amazement, it was a turtle, at least a foot across the top of the shell. My dogs started barking and were jumping up and down, thinking I was going to rescue them yet another friend. I pulled over as there was no traffic at the time. I got out and looked at the turtle and grabbed a stick to see if it was a snapping turtle. It was! And did he snap! I knew I could not safely pick up this turtle. A car pulled up behind mine and a man and his family, complete with three kids were in total awe of this amazing creature. The turtle was trying to cross the interstate but was headed toward the concrete barrier. The man went over to the turtle, asked me "where would you like him ma'am?" and proceeded to pick up the turtle. I said let's put him down the embankment. And off the turtle went. Probably to find the nearest swamp!

Ellie Rose

Ellie Rose

The Black Lab who was always dressed for fine dining
in her little tuxedo with five black buttons

Ellie Rose was adopted from a shelter at five weeks of age, too soon to be weaned. I had to decide between her and another Black Lab puppy. The shelter lady told me Ellie followed her everywhere and was very outgoing. That helped with my decision. Although I called her a Black Labrador Retriever, I was told she had some Springer Spaniel in her as she had white on her chest that included five black buttons, hence her little tuxedo keeping her always dressed for fine dining. Awaiting our latest adoption, was my second German Shepherd Rosie. Ellie waddled when she walked and her little tuxedo shook, making her even cuter than she already was as a high-energy puppy. Greeting her at the door was Rosie. My first German Shepherd Rebel had recently gone to Doggie Heaven and Rosie needed a new job—caring for a young puppy. Ellie was raised by Rosie and identified herself more as a German Shepherd than a Black Labrador Retriever. Rosie made my job as a new puppy owner easy. Ellie was Rosie's little shadow. She was intelligent and was quickly potty trained. I took both of my dogs everywhere and they both loved the water. It was a toss up who enjoyed playing ball or swimming more, my Lab or my Shepherd. One day while boating, Ellie stayed in the water and as we started up the boat and began to move, she swam so hard and fast as if to say "Wait for me! Wait for me!" The vet said Ellie was precocious! That was an understatement. She also had one white toenail. So when I clipped her nails, I would always tell her at shampoo and nail clipping time, "You need a shampoo and pedicure, particularly that one white toenail!" She always enjoyed her shampoos, but I am not sure if she enjoyed being told she had one white toenail. Ellie Rose, a Black Labrador Retriever who thought of herself as a German Shepherd, thanks to Rosie (her adopted Mom).

The Black Lab who was
always dressed for fine dining
in her little tuxedo
with five black buttons

Amazing Grace
Our Littlest Hero

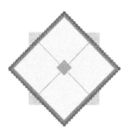

Amazing Grace

Belle

Maggie

MeMe

Sir Goldie Gandhi van Gogh

Ellie Rose

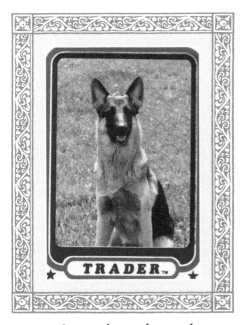

Rosie on her trading card

Sami One

Sami Two

Sami Two

Smokey Smiff (Smith)

Clover Honey—"Sir Honey"

Golden Autumn

Chloe Spice One

Chloe Spice Two

Zeus (left) and Buddy (right)

Brady

Brady

Brady

Buddy

Samantha

Cinnamon Spice (middle)

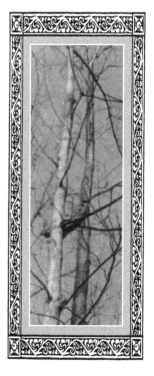

Lila Jewell

Tabitha

Calico

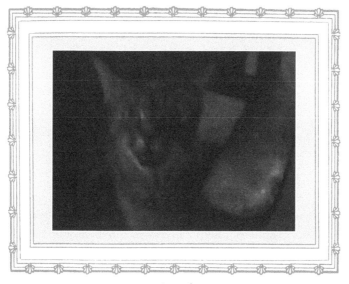

Hagatha

Maggie

Maggie, Friend LaLa, Chloe Spice, Tabitha

Miranda

Rosie (left) and Rebel (right)

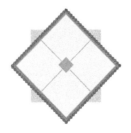

Amazing Grace
Our Littlest Hero

Rebel

The 100 pound German Shepherd pet therapy dog,
showing people how to love

I acquired my first German Shepherd (Rebel) and Rosie from
a professional breeder. I want to emphasize that this woman was
a professional breeder, not a backyard breeder! This woman had
been breeding German Shepherds for over 30 years, most of which
became show dogs, police dogs, military dogs, service and therapy
dogs. The definition of a professional breeder is that they do it to
better the breed, trying to "breed out" ailments common to that
particular breed, i.e., hip dysplasia, deafness, temperament, etc. This
woman had become a dear friend and treated her dogs like gold.
You could barely walk in her kitchen as there were dogs all over. Not
all of her dogs were "show" dogs. This was rare, but one particular
dog caught my attention as he was into everything, causing all kinds
of commotion. I adopted Rebel, not rescued, as these dogs were
never abused. While some people disagree and say to never buy
from a professional breeder, I do not agree. I have had purebreds
and "mutts". I have never experienced any difference as I have found
them to all be wonderful companions. Rebel was adopted as a
puppy and he quickly lived up to his name. All muscle, strong and
intelligent, Rebel was very intimidating to people. He did not always
like other dogs, particularly the high-pitched barking ones, but he
loved people and kids. I did day care with him and my kids would
lay on top of him and take their naps. He was always surrounded by
kids and felines as well as my second German Shepherd Rosie. Pet
therapy dogs were almost unheard of at the time I adopted Rebel
and at this time, German Shepherds were the "chosen" breed to
be targeted as fierce and mean. Rebel was my first Shepherd but I
always thought of them as heroes and so beautiful and intelligent.
Rebel was a puppy when I adopted him. He soon grew to weigh
more than me at the time. I took him everywhere with me which

included lots of travel. While working in day care, I got to know more than one family where the kids had been "taught" to fear animals, dogs, large dogs and of course, German Shepherds. Rebel would change all of that. We went into people's homes and with his love, patience and gentleness, he re-trained parents as well as kids that with a little respect and lots of love, dogs can be our best friends at least most of the time. He seemed to know what his job was as he pranced into homes, licked the kids and sat at attention awaiting his next command. We volunteered in the local elementary school and taught pet safety and how to be a responsible pet owner too. While living in a townhouse, he was restricted to staying in a large bedroom when I was at work. Upon arriving home, I noticed he was always out loose in the house. I knew I had closed the door. We left the house one morning and waited at the door. We saw Rebel come bounding down the stairs. He had opened the door. There was no holding him back. He was too intelligent for me! After that, he had free roam of the house. One day I had stopped at a convenience store. I had a little car that had a stick shift. A customer came in and asked who owned the little blue car in the parking lot. I had parked on a little slope and I looked out and it was rolling down the parking lot. I ran out, jumped in and stopped it just in time to stop it from hitting another car. There was Rebel sitting in the driver's seat. He had released the emergency brake with his paw. Every place I went, I took Rebel and Rosie, my second German Shepherd. Every time I left the car with them in it, Rebel always sat in the driver's seat and Rosie was always in the passenger seat. This got more than a few laughs. One time I left my purse in the car with a peanut butter cup in it. When I came back out, my purse had been unzipped, I found a nail size of the orange paper and Rebel had peanut butter breath. While chocolate is toxic to pets, Rebel was unfazed, fortunately this time. I never carried chocolate with me again! He also teethed on socks. Rebel and Rosie hiked in the mountains and one time our car would not start and it was getting cold. I huddled with my dogs to keep warm until help arrived. Rebel traveled with me often and I always felt protected. He was trained that if a driver was "tailgating" us, I would say "Rebel, we got ourselves a tailgater". He proceeded to sit up in the back seat and put his head in the back window. Every driver but one backed off. I guess they would rather not deal with him if they hit us. Rebel also saved my life five times, but that's another story.

Rosie on her trading card

Rosie

A "Pets on Wheels" dog, and little league mascot—with
her own trading card—position "catcher"

Rosie was my second German Shepherd and adopted from the same professional breeder as Rebel. Rosie was team mascot for the local little league team and a "pets on wheels" dog. She acquired quite the reputation as being kind, gentle, patient and so much a "people" dog, you would wait for her to actually starting talking human talk. I took her with me almost everywhere I went, including to offices. One of our twice-weekly duties included visiting the residents at our local nursing home. We visited the seniors on a regular basis. Rosie was definitely a "people" dog. She made the rounds and visited as many people as she could. It was very difficult to get her to say we'll be back in a few days. I think the seniors and Rosie had tears in their eyes. For the residents, Rosie and I may have been the only company they ever had. I strongly encourage people to visit residents in nursing homes, talk to the director and see what you can do to get your pet recognized as a "pets on wheels" dog or cat. An animal can make all the difference in a person's life, especially to those who are homebound, be it a nursing home, assisted living, adult foster care or in their own home. They may not be able to own a pet anymore, but they still love them. It's the best therapy for the pet and the resident.

Rosie was also team mascot for our local little league team. Rosie always seemed to know when it was time to "play ball!". She never missed a game in over four years. During one game, she ran into the outfield, retrieved the ball and the umpire was yelling "Get that dog off the field!" I screamed back "That's not a dog. That's Rosie!" The crowd roared and Rosie even took the ball to home plate. After that, Rosie was awarded the great honor of being the "catcher". When it came time for team pictures, Rosie was asked to pose. Because I had already taken a few hundred pictures of her at home, she would see the camera and sit at attention and look directly into the camera. On team picture day, there were over 100 kids awaiting for their pictures to be taken, individually and with their teams. The photographer was a professional and had done this for decades. When it came time for our team to get their picture taken, there was Rosie, sitting patiently waiting for the photographer. With all the kids running, yelling, jumping and doing what little leaguers do, Rosie sat perfectly still and looked directly into the camera. Even the photographer said he had never seen anything like this in his career. She got her own trading card (see photo section), complete with title of "Catcher", height, name and team. Awesome! Absolutely Awesome! But not amazing, because this was Rosie—team mascot, "pets on wheels" member and overall best friend in the world!!

I must add that when Rebel went to Doggie Heaven, Rosie grieved so hard, she barely ate for months. I thought I was going to lose her too. Please remember, pets grieve too. So give them special attention when their fellow animal friends go to Heaven. Hug them a little more often at this special time!

Buuuuuuuud!

*An Old English Sheepdog, matted, beaten and afraid
and one courageous rescuer*

I was traveling with my Black Labrador Retriever, Ellie Rose and my second German Shepherd Rosie. I was staying with some friends who had a huge log cabin in the woods. My dogs and I were hiking around the property one day when a beautiful Old English Sheepdog came bounding up to us, or at least I thought he was an Old English Sheepdog. It was very difficult to tell because he was matted so badly and dirty, his white fur was almost black. He was very scared and timid, clearly an abused animal. My dogs welcomed him with open paws and I calmly talked to him. I could tell from the look in his beautiful eyes he was begging for help and not just with his physical condition. We walked back to my friend's home where I gave him some cool water and a little food. He then got a bath. It took about two hours and the water was black and filled with gravel and dirt. He still was not clean but was better than before. His fur was matted so bad that his skin was growing around and into his fur. I went to town and bought baby scissors, the ones where the ends are round and not pointed. I could not even brush his fur it was matted so badly. I knew this was going to be a long process, but de-matting him was the only way to save this poor frightened creature. We sat on the porch for the next nine hours. We stopped for potty breaks and a little walk and more water. He never flinched and I was sweating profusely afraid I would cut his skin. I only "nicked" him once and he never moved. He was not restrained and my dogs just sat and watched, knowing we were saving yet another abused animal. Nine hours later, he was bald, down to the skin. He got another bath and this time he actually smiled at the relief of getting his fur cut off and being clean. And of course, he got lots of pats and love all the while. I let him stay on the porch for a quick nap and took my dogs for another little hike. I went back to my friend's home with my dogs and there waiting for us was the Old English Sheepdog. Because I was visiting and didn't know the area, I contacted the local veterinarian and asked where I could take this beautiful creature so he could find his forever home. They recommended an animal rescue shelter near town so off we went. This dog was amazing! He sat perfectly still in my car, surrounded by my two dogs. He was truly thankful for being rescued. I learned later that he had found his forever home, complete with little kids and a kind and loving family. We named him Buuuuuuuuuuuuuuud! He truly was a Bud!

A Baby Barred Owl

*A cardboard box and a teenager
the owl thought was his Dad*

I was vacationing at a friend's home for the summer and got to know the neighborhood kids as they visited often to play with my two dogs, my Black Labrador Retriever, Ellie Rose and my second German Shepherd Rosie. All of a sudden, I heard kids hollering and yelling at the top of their lungs. They came pounding on the front door and certainly got my attention quickly. I could barely understand what they were saying or should I say yelling, but finally figured out that there was a baby Barred Owl that had fallen out of its nest at one of their homes. I quickly retrieved my pet carrier that I keep on hand for rescues. Off we went with about six kids showing me the way as fast as we could run. I explained to them that they had to calm down as we did not want to scare the little owl more than he probably already was after his latest adventure. We approached the tree where his nest was located very slowly, quietly and carefully. The Momma owl was no where in sight. We spotted the owl laying on the ground. He appeared to be unhurt, but certainly a little scared and startled. Normally I would not touch or handle a wild animal as sometimes the Momma will reject the baby if she smells human scent on it and I could get bitten. However, this rescue required immediate attention and because the Momma owl was not around, I very softly and soothingly spoke to the baby owl. He had huge eyes and started flapping his little wings. They did not appear to be broken, but I knew he could not survive on his own. With lots of tender loving care, I picked up the tiny creature and put him in my pet carrier. He immediately responded by flapping his wings even faster. I was concerned he would go into shock or hurt himself or both. I walked quickly but gently back to my friend's home where I was vacationing. Not being from the area, I did not know of any rescue groups, so I called the local veterinarian. They put me in touch with a wildlife rescue and rehabilitation group in St. Louis, Missouri, which was about 45 minutes away. I got a large cardboard box as my carrier was too small and with flapping wings, I wanted to give my new found feathered friend as much room as possible, while still keeping him secure for his drive into town. With a neighborhood Mom and her teenage son holding the cardboard box on his lap and wearing huge dark "aviator-type" sunglasses, off we went to the city to find the wildlife refuge group who said they would take in our little feathered friend. The young man talked to the little creature and the baby owl, who had the biggest, roundest eyes I had ever seen, blinked at him every few seconds and by the look on his face, as if asking, "are YOU my Dad"? It was absolutely hysterical and very calming for the owl. With the big, dark sunglasses the young man was wearing and the big, dark eyes the owl had (and they appeared to be rolling as he blinked), I really think the owl thought he had been rescued by a much bigger owl, his Dad. We got to the wildlife rescue group and off the little owl went to his new home, to grow a little bigger and I learned later to be released into the wild! I had to research what a Barred Owl is and they do in fact have a white bar across their tail. When I tell people, they think I am saying a Barn Owl, but this fine, feathered creature was in fact a Barred Owl. So when rescuing a wild animal, follow all the safety rules and try to locate your nearest wildlife rescue group.

A cardboard box and
a teenager the owl thought
was his Dad

Sami One

AMAZING GRACE, Our Littlest Hero

Sami One

*The German Shepherd who met Lucy Doe Deer
at the bus stop, and played snow soccer*

Sami "One" was my third German Shepherd. I never thought I could have yet another wonderful Shepherd.

My first two German Shepherds I had gotten from a friend of mine when they were just puppies. They both had such beautiful temperaments, great with other dogs, kids and of course protective, but not aggressive—the perfect dog. After my Black Labrador Retriever went to Doggie Heaven, I knew I had to honor her and adopt another dog, plus I just could not live without a dog as I have had dogs since I was a kid. I was at the vet one day and saw a picture of a German Shepherd, whose owner had recently gone to Heaven and this dog was in need of a loving home. I stared at her picture and prayed, asking God if this was the dog for me. The answer was simple—of course, why ask. I called the people, got directions to their home where they had this beautiful canine and off I went.

When I arrived, this beautiful dog was outside playing ball. All I could think was her picture on the bulletin board at the vet did not do her justice. She was so far more beautiful and ravishing than any picture could have shown. The caretakers were throwing balls on the roof and as they came down, the dog jumped into the air and retrieved them. What an amazing animal. I wondered how many humans could do that. The dog ignored me when I tried to talk to her and only wanted to play ball.

I was so focused on this dog that I was ignoring the caretakers. I looked at them for a couple of minutes and realized we had worked together a few years ago. They told me the history of this dog and her owner. The owner was a senior and had recently gone to Heaven and they wanted to make sure this dog got the best possible home. I already had a list of references for these people including my veterinarian. No need. They knew me and they knew I had been rescuing forever.

I grabbed a tennis ball and started throwing the ball and that was all I had to do to become friends with MY new best friend. I was going to school to work with a class of first graders. I was so trusting of this dog that I took her with me and she was immediately introduced to about 25 kids. Hugs, kisses, more hugs and more kisses, I am not sure who got more, her or the kids she met. This was yet another perfect German Shepherd for me. Trustworthy, yet protective.

I stopped at the store and bought tennis balls and went home. Before we even went in the house, I was throwing balls up on the roof for her and she was jumping two feet in the air, sometimes higher to retrieve her new toys. She even brought the balls over to me and when I said drop it, she immediately dropped it at my feet, only to wait anxiously for the next tennis ball to fall off of the roof.

This was in September and winter soon became a reality for us. I knew if I didn't play ball with her, she would be depressed, so much to my amazement, I discovered that even on the coldest winter days, with snow over 3 feet deep, if I threw the ball, she would dive into huge snow banks and bring me the ball. When it was icy, I was worried about her hurting herself. She would not take no for an answer so off we went to the driveway, ice covered complete with snow. Not surprising, she did not care if it was 5 degrees out and the snow was taller than she was. I threw her tennis balls and should would slip and slide, but always bring me her tennis balls. One day, I started throwing more than one ball at a time, and off she went to bring them back, first one, then the other.

I always told her she should have been a goalie on a hockey team.

So this perfect dog, smart, beautiful, protective, developed a new game—Playing snow soccer with Sami.

When we were not playing ball, Sami was my constant companion. Her biggest job was to walk with me to and from the bus stop to drop off in the morning and pick up in the afternoon a couple of neighborhood kids. One day, when walking, I noticed what I thought was a funny looking tree. The closer we got, the more I realized that this was not a tree at all. It was in fact an adult deer, a doe. Sami started barking loudly and the deer did not move. I thought at first she must be sick, but she was very healthy and

I think she knew Sami would not hurt her. The closer we got, the more Sami barked and the deer still did not move. When the kids and Sami and I were about 10 feet from this beautiful deer, she very slowly walked across the dirt road into the woods. The kids asked me if they could go see the deer. I said sure. They got so close to her, they could have touched her nose. The deer never moved. She stood perfectly still and let the kids talk to her all the while Sami was still barking.

The next day, at the same time and the same place, this little show was reenacted again, I am sure for the sheer delight of the two neighborhood kids going to the bus stop, with Sami close at their sides. This time, we decided to give our new found friend a name, Lucy Doe Deer. We never saw this particular deer again, however the next Spring, we saw a fawn and there is no doubt that this was Lucy Doe Deer's new baby.

P.S. When I got Sami, she was already ten years old. When she went to Doggie Heaven, she was 14 and still playing balls and snow soccer and in dog years at 14, she would be 98 years old. If only we humans could do these amazing feats at that age!

Sami Two

Sami Two

*She's beautiful, ravishing and intelligent
and absolutely brilliant! And she knows it!*

After my third German Shepherd Sami One went to Doggie
Heaven, I was pitiful, just pitiful. I just had to get another Shepherd.
I always tell people that while we cannot replace our pets, we can
adopt in their honor. It was shortly after Christmas, snow still on
the ground, but we had a few warm days. I would go for walks,
but without my four-legged friend at my side. I called my vet to
see if anyone had a Shepherd looking for a home, looked in the
newspaper and asked friends. There were no available dogs at
this time. I posted an ad on "Craigs List" and within ten minutes,
I received a response. I called the people who said they had an
awesome Shepherd and they needed to place her in a nice home.
I drove only about 15 minutes and upon arrival, as I was walking
into their home, I knew this was the dog for me and I had not even
met her yet. There were six kids, all ages, from a baby crawling on
the floor to elementary school aged kids sitting on the sofa.
There were cats all over too. The kids hollered, "we know you!"
I recognized them from my local school where I volunteered. The
lady came over, introduced herself and asked if I wanted to see the
dog. "Of course!" I said. Out came a full-grown German Shepherd,
bold, beautiful and while jumping over the baby on the floor, she
proceeded to lick the other kids and was begging someone, anyone
to play with her. The rest is history. I could tell her temperament
and energy was just what I was looking for. I really did not believe
I could find yet another Shepherd so wonderful as I had previously
owned. We went to the local store and purchased several tennis
balls. My other Shepherd lived to chase tennis balls, thrown in the
air, rolled down the driveway or thrown on the roof and bouncing
off her nose or being caught by her, no matter the weather, the
temperature, she was up for a good game of "tennis". And it was

true, we started off by playing "tennis". She jumps three feet into the air and does twists and she chases her tennis balls. In winter, she "snaps" at the falling snow and digs deep to retrieve her tennis balls. She is perfect. And every day with Sami Two is another blessed day for me, another blessed day for her. I trained her to stay on our property and she goes everywhere with me (weather permitting). She loves, adores and sometimes just tolerates the cats I have. Sometimes, they snuggle with her, sometimes they play with her ears, sometimes they groom her, sometimes she grooms them. But always, they love each other. The neighborhood kids adore her and ask to play with her. When the sprinkler is on, she attacks the water. We have only replaced the sprinkler twice so far this year.

She also rolls over daily for "tummy rubs". She is beautiful, ravishing, intelligent and absolutely brilliant! And I tell her this every day!

Sami Two

Smokey Smiff (Smith)

Smokey Smiff (Smith)

The gad about cat who loved the big, burly guys
at the maintenance garage

Smokey Smith was yet another fabulous feline I had not planned on getting. I was reading the classifieds in our local paper and while I usually don't go to the free pets section, I did this day. The ad read: Gray and white cat, found, can't keep, stressing out my dog, needs good home fast!

I knew what happened to this type of animal—they must be adopted soon or they would be taken to the shelter or worse. I called the phone number listed, talked to the lady who had Smokey, went to her home and laughable as it was, there was Smokey, sitting prim and proper, looking at the outside world through the sliding glass door. A few feet away was the lady's dog, little, yapping, barking and charging at Smokey, who didn't even flinch. I thought that's hysterical. The ad said the cat was stressing out the dog. It certainly appeared the dog was stressing out herself as the cat was totally ignoring the dog.

The lady and I chatted for a while and my instinct was right, I must adopt Smokey today. I took him home where he was welcomed with open paws by my other cats and dog. He was clearly Siamese with a Siamese meow, slender and when he walked, he was definitely strutting his stuff. He looked like he was walking on his tippy toes, with a very refined look about him, like royalty.

At this time, as we lived in the country, I still let my cats out to play. I let Smokey adjust but eventually he was allowed to explore the outside world. One day he didn't come home. I was very worried, so I called my local newspaper and placed a lost ad. To my amazement, someone else had just called the paper with a found ad. They had found Smokey.

We have a boarding school not too far from my home, so I grabbed my pet carrier and rode my bike to the maintenance garage.

I knew some of the guys working there as they had helped me with live traps for previous rescues. As I walked into the garage, with trucks larger than my home and guys who looked like they worked out every day, actually they did with their jobs, I saw cans of tuna all over the garage floor and there was Smokey, eating away. I thanked the guys for rescuing him and some of them truly did not want to let him come back home with me. They had fallen in love with a 5 pound Siamese fabulous feline.

I still did not want to keep Smokey inside all the time, so I let him out one more time with my other kitties. This time, I kept an extra good eye on him and watched where he was going exploring. This time he was making his way through the woods to a friends home. He approached their yard and to my total amazement, he jumped up in a lounge chair. A teenage girl came out and in her hands, she had canned cat food. There was Smokey, the gad about kitty, being served in his lounge chair. If only every cat had such a life.

I retrieved Smokey and unhappy as he was with my decision, Smokey was kept indoors from then on as it was too dangerous for him to leave home. He was however, treated to "fine dining" in my home, his forever home.

Smokey Smiff (Smith)

Clover Honey — "Sir Honey"

Clover Honey — "Sir Honey"

*The tourists' morning coffee companion
who was written about in guest books*

Another cat in the neighborhood—from where he came, nobody knows. He just appeared as did a lot of strays. People were dumping them and or strays always know to come to people who love them. They have a sixth sense, if they are lucky and don't find themselves in harm's way first. A dear friend of mine had two houses in our neighborhood, one she lived in and one she rented to tourists. There was a guest book at the rental and it soon became apparent that there was a "stray" cat who was definitely a "people" cat. We started reading comments left in the guestbook by the guests that said things like "This cat jumped on my lap as I was drinking my morning coffee". "Where did you get this one cat who keeps me company in the morning as I sit and look at the lake?" "What is the cat's name who sits on the chair on the front porch as I enjoy my breakfast?" My friend was keeping an eye out for this cat as no one knew who he was. One day, a huge orange and white, long-haired cat appeared on MY door step. It had to be HIM! I called my friend who came over and we took him inside my house. He did not have a name. I was in the kitchen and I had honey on the counter, in the little bear. It was "Clover" Honey. So with kitty's orange coloring, he was officially named Clover Honey. With his reputation of keeping the tourists company for their morning coffee, he was knighted Sir Honey. As the tourist season ended and the rental was closed for winter, Sir Honey was adopted by the "zoo" and lived with us until the next tourist season. Whoever said cats are aloof, I have never experienced that, although I am sure some can be shy and tend to stay away from some humans. That is something that does not happen at my house. My cats are "people" cats and cannot get enough attention.

Golden Autumn

Golden Autumn

*Rescued from a dungeon who saw
the golden leaves of autumn for the first time*

I was working in a box store and developed a friendship with a co-worker. One day she came to me, after learning I do almost anything for an animal. She shared a gut-wrenching story of yet another fabulous feline. An acquaintance of hers had a cat that lived in his "workshop". At least that is what he said. As my friend got more information, this "workshop" was actually a dungeon with no light, no windows, and an area of about 16 square feet. After a month of chatting with this person, I knew it would not be easy to get his cat away from him. While his definition of loving an animal is far different from mine, he really did not see anything wrong or inhumane or cruel in keeping this cat in these living conditions. He thought with a little food and some water, that's all a cat required. One day, after work, I approached him. Something just told me to go ask directly for the cat. While I have no patience with people like this, I know I will never get the animal if I approach the person in anger. So quietly, gently and with understanding, I asked if I could get the cat after work and let him join my zoo. I was shocked at how receptive he was to the idea. I waited until he got off work and went to the house (with a friend). I never go alone as this is not safe for me or anyone. Always! Take a friend with you. As I pulled into the driveway, I was stunned! The house was beautiful, huge, at least five bedrooms with LOTS of room. All I could think of was this poor animal living in a dungeon. I was invited in and walked to the dungeon. As he opened the door, I saw this long-haired, majestic creature, squinting at me. I could barely see my hand in front of my face. I very carefully walked up to the cat. He did not flinch and seemed to be relieved to see another human, a good human. Animals know these things! I picked him up, held him tight, thanked the owner and walked to the car.

Sitting on my friend's lap, we drove away and I thanked God with all my heart. I dropped off my friend and went home. It was Fall. The leaves were just turning colors and falling from the trees. I had not even thought of a name for this incredible, gentle creature. I got out of the car, held my new friend and as I bent down to unlock my door, while looking at leaves and shading my kitty's eyes from the sunlight as he was squinting, his name became "Golden Autumn". Golden Autumn saw the sunshine for the first time in years, he was golden as his heart was pure as is every animal's heart. I said "Look Goldie. These are the leaves. This is the sunshine. This is the world. Look! Goldie". We rustled the leaves, his eyes adjusted and he lived happily ever after while enjoying the sunshine, the world and all the love my zoo could give him, never to be put in a dungeon again.

Golden Autumn

Chloe Spice One

Chloe Spice One

Screeching from a dog crate
"It's me! It's me! I'm over here!"

The phone rang. Another animal in distress. This time, it was rescued by a couple who lived on a farm not too far away. They could not keep kitty and had put her in a dog crate—imagine a CAT being put in a DOG crate—how humiliating. Just kidding! They gave me vague directions to their farm house, simply telling me it was a white farm house on such and such road and the cat is in the dog crate. I barely knew where they were. Driving slowly down the country road, grateful there was no traffic, I kept looking for a dog crate on a front porch. My window was rolled down and I am glad it was. Suddenly, screeching, I heard a cat wailing at the top of her little lungs! I know she was saying "It's me! It's me! I'm over here!" I pulled over to the side of the road, waiting for more wailing and followed the sound. There on the front porch of a white farm house was a huge dog crate with a light-colored calico kitty wailing at me. She knew I was there to retrieve her. Animals know these things! I went to the crate, opened the door, petted her, and quickly put her in my carrier. She was not afraid, very gentle and grateful to be out of the DOG crate! I never met the people who rescued her initially. And yes, we can talk to the animals—if we only listen carefully, we will understand them!

Chloe Spice Two

AMAZING GRACE, Our Littlest Hero

Chloe Spice Two

*A horrific thunderstorm, lots of tuna
and one scared but tenacious rescuer*

Several years ago, some neighbors moved and of course abandoned their kitty. They knew me and I knew them, and while they did not tell me what they had done, word got around. I went to their empty house and there was kitty, a short-haired light-colored calico. I also peeked in the windows to make sure there were no other abandoned pets. Timid and shy, this kitty was too scared to be an easy rescue. She would not come to me so I went home, got a bowl for water, took lots of tuna with me including a can opener. I sat on the back steps of the empty house for several nights. I could see her in the woods and hear her tiny meows. She would not come close to me. She was several yards away and I knew she was very hungry. I left a little tuna on the steps when I went home at night. I did not leave lots of tuna as I did not want her to get "full" on tuna and never come to me. Finally on the last night of my rescue attempt, it began to rain and thunder. Even though I am not fond of storms, I waited for her. I made sure I was safe from lightning, waited for kitty and with the open can of tuna, she came to within a few feet of me. I sat on the top step of about four. She was close enough for me to touch her. I moved the wrong way and bumped the can, making a scraping sound on the steps. She jumped, I jumped and off she ran into the woods. I went home in tears thinking I had scared her so badly, she would never come near me. The next day, this scene was reenacted, however this time the weather was good. Sitting on the top step with tuna in hand, here came kitty. Apparently, her hunger outweighed her fear and as I always say, animals know the good humans. She came up to the top step and to my total amazement, I reached down, petted her and picked her up, put her in my carrier and took her to her forever home.

Zeus (left) and Buddy (right)

Zeus

*Thrown into a cornfield and driven 200 miles
to her forever home, lived to be over 20 years old*

Zeus lived 20 years and four months. A neighbor wanted another
kitty as her missionary work was coming to an end. She had traveled
around the world but now was a home body and wanted the
company of a kitty. Zeus came into my life as I answered the phone
one evening to someone I had never met. They were driving about
200 miles from home and saw a car pull over and throw something
out the window. It was a kitten, a small gray kitten. The kitten was
retrieved from the cornfield, miraculously unharmed. Weighing
about 3 pounds, with huge green eyes, the kitten sat on the lap of
the passenger in the car for the next four hours. While still near the
cornfield, these people called me and asked if I could take in yet
another fabulous feline. I said only if they drove it to me, which they
did. Pure gray, slender, short-haired and timid, Zeus entered my
life. My dogs welcomed her and my other cats asked her what HER
story was as they all had their own stories to tell. Sniffing, licking
and purring, the other cats helped Zeus adjust. Being a kitten,
adjustment was not difficult. Animals just want to be loved and she
was grateful she lived through flying into a cornfield with no wings.
Zeus lived with us for several years until my neighbor saw her. I let
Zeus go live with my neighbor who already had rescued another
kitty a few years ago. Zeus, now almost 20 years old, is still happy,
healthy and grateful someone was in the right place at the right time
and saw her being thrown from a car into a cornfield, only to be
driven 200 miles to her new-found home.

Brady

AMAZING GRACE, Our Littlest Hero

Brady Barney Buttons

*Abandoned, awesome, loves to be brushed
and lives to give hugs*

I received a call from friends who lived in a local apartment complex. The management had allowed pets for years, but all of a sudden, pets were no longer allowed. The result of this new policy for the pet owners and particularly the pets was heartbreaking, to say the least. Hundreds of pets were suddenly homeless, with pet owners scrambling to find them homes. On the other end of the phone, was a frantic friend who had rescued several cats, but there was one left that she could not find a home for—a short-haired gray, de-clawed, neutered huge fabulous feline. With big green eyes, crying for a new home and desperate to be loved, was Brady. Probably middle aged, the owners could not be located. My friend thought they had moved and just left their pet behind. Another abandoned kitty, left to fend for himself and at the mercy of humans. Thankfully, my friend was an animal lover and kept the kitty in her apartment at the risk of being in trouble with management. She told me there was no way she was going to dump this kitty. Therefore, she called me to see if I could take in yet another critter. And of course, I said yes. My friend and her husband said they would be over soon and the next thing I knew, in came kitty in a huge cardboard box. He jumped out of the box and was the biggest kitty I had ever owned. He appeared to be in good health. He was friendly and very affectionate. He immediately stood on his hind legs and crawled up my arm to literally put his front paws around my shoulders and gave me a huge hug, I knew this kitty had not been mistreated. He was simply left behind because of the new "no pets" policy at his former apartment complex. My other pets welcomed him with open paws, as they always did. Brady acted like he had already been in his new home forever. He was kind, gentle and loved his fellow critter family immediately. The next morning

Brady

as I was drying my hair, Brady proceeded to jump on the counter and he demanded to have his hair brushed and dried with my hair dryer. Normally, animals don't like the noise of a hair dryer but with Brady, this became a daily ritual. He knew where my brush was kept and every morning, he was on the counter waiting for his beauty makeover. He has since taught two other fabulous felines the morning drill and they too are on the counter waiting to be brushed but Brady is always first. Whenever friends visit, Brady jumps on the closest chair he can find, stands on his hind legs and proceeds to crawl up the person's arm and literally hug them. Some people are amazed. But knowing Brady, I am used to it, and look forward to my feline hugs!

An Algae Eater

Thrown from a third floor balcony
while in his fish tank

I was visiting a young couple who lived in an apartment. They lived on the second floor. Each apartment had balconies except the lower level had patios. Sitting on the sofa, chatting and enjoying their young children, we heard lots of noise, loud voices and a lot of commotion coming from the third floor apartment. My friends told me these people were moving! The next thing we knew, we saw a fish tank, complete with water, gravel and fish toys, come flying down from their balcony, landing on the ground below. We rushed to the balcony and saw what remained of the fish tank, blue gravel all over the ground and something huge and black quivering on the ground. My friend was screaming "That's an algae eater! That's an algae eater! It's alive!" I ran to the kitchen, grabbed a big empty jar, put water in it and my friend was already outside picking up the algae eater. It was miraculously uninjured but breathing rapidly. My friend called her Dad, who had a huge fish tank. She drove while I held the algae eater in the jar of water. The algae eater, who remains nameless, was quickly introduced to its new home, complete with lots of finned friends. So for this algae eater in need of a speedy rescue, one person or should I say a few in this instance, can make all the difference!

Thrown from a third floor balcony
while in his fish tank

A Little White Mouse, a Curious Kitten and Christmas Carols in August

Meow Meow the mouse who lived
to rock in his hamster wheel

I was visiting friends who had a kitten, a little white mouse and a four year old child. We had left the child with a babysitter and walked into town for a little sightseeing. I knew the mouse was in a cage in the house and the kitten had free run of the house—not a good combination. The child was a true animal lover and had no clue that you don't allow a kitten to be "friends" with a mouse. The next thing we knew, the babysitter and the child came running down the street calling our names. The babysitter was visibly upset and was trying hard not to scare the child who was not really aware of what the commotion was all about. The babysitter proceeded to tell us the child had let the mouse out of its cage and the kitten had the mouse cornered in the bathroom behind the door. Never having run this fast in my life, my friend, babysitter and child in tow, must have looked quite comical politely pushing and shoving our way around people. Up two flights of stairs we bounded. I held my breath as I looked behind the bathroom door, fearing the worst. The little mouse was in shock with a little spot of blood on it, but with no other visible signs of injury. The cat was licking her chops a few feet away. I knelt down, picked up the tiny mouse, went to the kitchen sink and with gentle, warm water washed the blood off the little mouse, dried him and talked soothingly. I dried the little mouse and returned him to his cage, which included a hamster wheel. By this time, neighbor's kids had come over for dinner, unaware of what just transpired. It was August, and while I could not think of anything else to do but to let the little mouse recover, I began to sing the sweetest Christmas carols I knew. All the kids chimed in and before we knew it, the little mouse perked up, started doing what mice do with a hamster wheel. He began going round and round and round to our total amazement. The more we sang, the more active he became. We decided to name the little mouse Meow Meow. Talking, singing and clapping for him, he spun faster and faster in the hamster wheel. We eventually sat down for dinner and Meow Meow was truly the hero of the hour!

A Little Boy, his Beagle, a Bus Driver and a Busy Highway

I am not particularly fond of winter and especially winter driving. This day would be a new challenge for me and especially to a little boy and his beagle. Driving down a busy highway, with snow on both sides of the road, I spotted what I thought was a small boy, about 10 years old on his bike of all things trying to maneuver through traffic. I gasped, slowed way down, put my emergency lights on and suddenly on the side of the road, I spotted a very frightened beagle. The boy had a look of absolute panic on his face and the beagle was darting in and out of traffic. I thought for sure he was going to be hit by a car. I stopped in my lane and in the oncoming lane was a local bus. He too stopped, put on his emergency lights, so between the two of us, we had miraculously gotten traffic to stop. The boy got off his bike and started chasing his dog, who only ran faster, clearly not knowing which way to go. I screamed for the boy to get off the road! At this point, the dog ran toward the little boy, who got on his bike. I yelled at him that I never wanted to see him on this road again. He waved and with his little beagle running as fast as his little legs could go, the boy pedaled hard and fast in the direction of his home. I never saw either the boy or his beagle again. This process took about ten minutes. The bus driver was watching intently and at first I thought he was upset at this latest adventure, but as I started to get back into my car, he gave me a huge thumbs up. I waved and returned the gesture. Special thanks go to this driver, whom I never found out his name. A lot of patience and a lot of love saved this little boy and his beagle!

Cinnamon Spice (middle)

Cinnamon Spice

And a very dark and stormy night

I am not keen on thunderstorms, driving in them or watching them on t.v. Another call, another cat, dumped on the side of the road at night and during a really bad thunderstorm. I knew the road where I was going and I did not like it in daylight let alone on a very dark and stormy night. I was not even sure where the kitty was. It had been an hour since the people had first called me. Off I went, with the pet carrier in my car. With thunder and torrential rain, I pulled over in the vicinity of the kitty in question. There was no traffic, otherwise, it would have been far too dangerous to do this. I got out and was screaming "Kitty! Kitty! Kitty!" Out of the ditch and weeds, soaking wet, terrified, weak and very traumatized, this kitty came to me with no hesitation. I had only been there about five minutes. It was as if she was waiting for me. I put her in my carrier, we went home, I dried her with a towel and then my hair dryer. She shivered and I thanked God for yet another beautiful creature to welcome into my life. She was a dark-colored, short-haired calico, more cinnamon colors and her other colors of those of nutmeg and vanilla, hence the name Cinnamon Spice. She was adopted out to the neighbor where she lived in the lap of luxury as every animal should.

Buddy

A Little Black Squirrel who turned into a Little Black Kitten

It all started with a simple lunch break

I rarely take lunch breaks when out and about. But this day was different and full of surprises. I went to a local sandwich shop, bought a seafood sub and went to the local grocery store parking lot just to watch traffic go, listen to the radio and relax a bit before going home. I was parked at a very busy intersection, dangerous for someone in their car, let alone for an animal trying to cross the highway. I was observing the local gas station across the street. I saw something very tiny and black. I thought "Oh a little black squirrel". This "squirrel" moved differently than most squirrels. I looked closer and to my amazement, it was a little black kitten, maybe six weeks old. I put my sandwich down, buckled up, started my car and had to wait for traffic to clear to get out of the parking lot. I got over to the gas station and saw the kitten dodging cars. I knew this was not good. There are no houses nearby and I knew this kitten had been "dumped". I did not have my pet carrier with me and no kitten food, but I had my seafood sub. I went over to kitten who stopped where he was and did not even move. I reached down, grabbed kitty and put him in my car. He smelled my sandwich and was clearly starving. I gave him a piece of crabmeat. That was his introduction to his new home. So this was my lunch treat, a little black squirrel who turned into a little black kitten. "Buddy" is just that, Buddy to everyone and always into mischief!

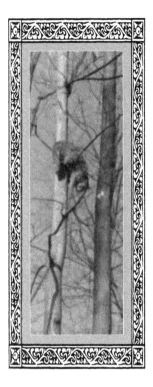

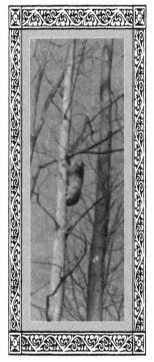

Lila Jewell

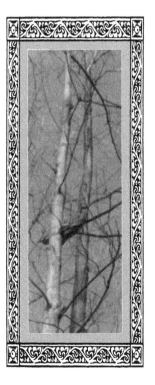

Lila Jewell

*A tree, a thunderstorm, a juicy, steaming hamburger
and seven days later*

"No! I'm not calling the fire department for a cat up a tree!" That
is what my neighbors kept telling me I should do. A small kitten,
probably two months old at most, was up a neighbor's tree, too
terrified to come down or even respond to any of the half a dozen
people who were trying to get her down. This was a very tall tree,
too dangerous to climb up and retrieve her. We all took turns trying
to coax her down from the tree, complete with smelly cat food,
tuna, talking and short of actually calling the fire department to
bring in a bucket truck, which we did not and would not have done
as our firefighters are busy saving lives, this kitten was not going
to cooperate with us. The more we called kitty, the more she went
further up an already tall tree. At one point, she went way out on a
narrow branch. I thought for sure she would fall. While people say
cats land on their feet, that is NOT true. Cats fall and get hurt too!
The sixth night she was in the tree, we had a mean thunderstorm.
Praying for her, I was hoping she would eventually come down.
The next morning, she was still there, soaking wet and shaking like
a leaf, pun intended. I went into the kitchen, fixed a hamburger and
stood under the tree with neighbors gawking and cheering for kitty
to come down. As the steam from the hamburger rose, I took my
hand and tried to make it go further up the tree and towards kitty.
It worked! She started climbing down. No one said a word, we were
all holding our breath. When kitty got close enough, I gave her a
taste of the hamburger, took her into my arms and brought her
inside. I dried her, fed her and again, she was welcomed into my
home with open paws! She never climbed this tree again.

Samantha

Samantha Rollie Pollie Panda Penguin Boogie Jewell

A long name for a very tiny bouncing kitten

While looking for garage sales, a friend and I found something we were not quite looking for on a bright, sunny day on a country road. We spotted something black and white, at first thinking it was a small skunk. Driving slowly, we came up to what was a very tiny kitten that was so small, he would fit in the palm of your hand. This kitten was not actually walking like kittens do, but was bouncing, one tiny hop at a time. His markings were unique. His face was round and looked like a panda, his chest looked like a penguin and down the right side of his face, there was a little black that looked like a "boogie". We looked around for houses, people or more kittens or the Momma cat. We found none. We retrieved the little tiny kitten and took him home. As he got older, his little body got rounder and rounder, he continued to bounce and his face became more "panda" like as time went on. Sometimes, he even waddled like a penguin. So for a very tiny kitten, Samantha Rollie Pollie Panda Penguin Boogie Jewell got a very big name.

Maggie

Maggie, Friend LaLa, Chloe Spice, Tabitha

Maggie

*A one-eyed kitten, the littlest of the bunch
and the bravest just like her Mom*

Maggie is one of Amazing Grace's kittens. She came with only one eye but you would never know it. She is just like her Mom, kind, gentle, intelligent and amazing. Although she is part of the "zoo", Maggie is in touch with every event, every critter and every detail of the house. She pays attention to all the other critters, making sure they stay in line. Whenever there is a ruckus, from any of them, Maggie is right there, right in the middle of things. Even with my German Shepherd, and although Maggie is not as big as my Shepherd's head, she is fearless. Actually she has given herself the title of the kitten "in charge". I guess you would call her the alpha kitten, although she is the littlest of the bunch. She never grew much, probably being the runt of the litter, but is in good health. And to look at her, you would never know she has only one eye. But that one eye keeps an eye, pun intended, on everything!

Tabitha

Calico

AMAZING GRACE, Our Littlest Hero

A Momma Kitty and Her Baby

Separated at the shelter and reunited at the shelter

While volunteering at the local animal shelter, although it was very difficult, it was something the animals looked forward to every day. I would take the cats out of their cages, pet them, talk to them and yearn to take them ALL home! One particular day, I was noticing a beautiful, short-haired dark calico kitty. I checked the date she came in. It was several days ago and she looked incredibly depressed and would not respond to me, no matter what I tried. I even held her and tried to cheer her up. She actually had a little tear coming down her cheek. I put her back in her cage and looked at the kitten in the cage above her. I read the date she was brought in and noticed it was the same date the older, depressed kitty had arrived. I asked a shelter worker what were these kitty's stories. He said the older, depressed kitty was the Momma cat and the kitten was hers. The Momma kitty was one year old, the kitten only a few weeks old. I asked why they were separated and emphasized how depressed the Momma kitty was. The worker told me they had to be separated so the kitten could be weaned. That answer was NOT good enough for me, so I proceeded to the front desk, completed the necessary paperwork to adopt BOTH of them. Off we went to their forever home. Today Momma kitty is 17 years old and her kitten is 16 years old, never to be separated again!

Hagatha

Hagatha

Known as "Haaaaaaaaaaaaaaaaaaagatha!"—
mouthy and magnificent!

Another phone call, another kitty. Nothing new. Except this kitty was sitting on the tail gate of a car in the local shopping center with people trying to give her away. A tiny tabby with an orange dot on her forehead I was told and a kitten meow that could be heard blocks away. The people were bragging that at home they would throw her up against a wall and laugh hysterically! Sickened and disgusted, my friend who called me did so from her cell phone while standing near the little kitten. Could I take her? Of course I would take her! My friend, with kitten in hand, arrived within minutes. We checked the kitten for broken teeth or bones. She seemed to be in good health and looked quite relieved to be in good, warm, loving hands. We named her Hagatha! She is quite the talker, and can carry on a long conversation. She is a far better listener than most people. She loves to talk! When opening her tiny mouth, her whiskers flare, and with the loudest meow I have ever heard, she "talks" to anyone who will listen. Yes, Hagatha is mouthy and magnificent and her conversations are always interesting and never boring!

Miranda

AMAZING GRACE, Our Littlest Hero

Miranda Gray Wolf White Tiger Ocelot Abyssinian Cougar Jewell

Abandoned in a hot, abandoned car

Miranda came to me as a tiny, barely weaned, short-haired kitten with multiple colors and markings, the most unusual I have ever seen for a domestic cat. Hence, she acquired the many names to describe her. White tiger markings, ocelot eyes and Abyssinian for breed recognition, gray wolf for her fur and colors, and cougar for her sleek, long body. The call came from a family member. Her older brother, a teenager, had been hiking in the woods with friends on an extremely hot summer day. The temperature was above 90, with humidity almost as bad. As they walked, they heard many animal sounds and at first they thought they were hearing a squirrel, an owl or possibly a cougar as there had been "sightings" in our area. They felt something was terribly wrong with this particular sound and followed it. They came upon an abandoned car, windows were rolled up tight and in the window, almost out of breath and panting, there was a tiny kitten, trying to screech, but there was no sound coming from her little lungs. The boys quickly found a rock and proceeded to knock out the window and retrieve the frail kitten. Relieved, terrified and weak, this fabulous feline collapsed into one of the boy's arms. One of the other boys called my friend and told her the story. She said bring kitty to her house immediately, but first get some fresh water for kitty, putting only a few drops of water in her tiny mouth while sprinkling a little on her over-heated body. Too much could kill her. She arrived shortly thereafter and was improving rapidly. Knowing it was just a matter of minutes she would have been dead in the abandoned car, we all felt like this kitty had a guardian angel that guided these wonderfully compassionate teenagers to her and saved her life. Not only would she have died from the heat in the car, she was dehydrated as well. I went to my friend's home and retrieved kitten. She immediately acquired her name as she represented so many other animals, from White Tigers to Cougars to Ocelots to Gray Wolves!

Volunteering at the local animal shelter

A Christmas fund raiser, a blizzard, and three cats later

Living in the upper Midwest we have some pretty harsh winters. As a volunteer at the local animal shelter, I was assigned to sales—sales of Christmas trees to raise money to help the animals. One bitterly cold and snowy winter night, while standing outside amongst many beautiful home-grown, local Christmas trees, I prayed a lot of them would be sold, but was doubtful as we were getting a blizzard with "white out" conditions. White out means you should stay home as you can barely see where you are driving. I went inside to get warm and visit the kitties. If any Christmas tree shoppers arrived they would ring the bell. I noticed three little forlorn kitties and thinking they would be alone for Christmas, I went to the front desk (again!), completed the necessary adoption paperwork and while I did not sell one Christmas tree that night, I brought home three fabulous felines. At first I was thinking the shelter got the better deal, having found homes for three cats in one night, but then of course, I knew better. I got the better deal with having yet three more fabulous feline friends to love. What an awesome, as in animals are awesome! Christmas present!

A Christmas fund raiser,
a blizzard,
and three cats later

AMAZING GRACE, Our Littlest Hero

Part Two

◆

Spaying and Neutering

Why it is So Important

Please Help Control the Pet Overpopulation.
Have Your Pet Spayed or Neutered!

Startling Statistics

Showing the Importance of Spaying and Neutering

Links are provided in "Spay/Neuter Organizations" to spay/neuter assistance programs and organizations. Just GOOGLE your area and you will find assistance.

FACTS/MYTHS

- The average number of litters a fertile cat produces is one to two a year; the average number of kittens is four to six per litter. The average number of litters a fertile dog produces is one a year; the average number of puppies is four to six.

- Number of cats and dogs born every day in the U.S. is 70,000.

- Almost 3,000 are born every hour or 50 are born every minute.

- Number of animals in the U.S. that die each year from cruelty, neglect, and exploitation: 30 million.

- Yearly cost to U.S. taxpayers to impound, shelter, euthanize and dispose of homeless animals: $2 billion.

- People do not spay/neuter because of money issues, time or getting the pet to the vet. Some people believe it's more fair to allow the cat to have kittens just once or they think a female cat's pregnancy and kittens will be so cute for the children to see or may even think it's educational.

DID YOU KNOW?. . .

- Cats can start mating as early as six months

- Even indoor-only house cats often find ways to get outdoors when the sexual urge hits them. Whether they disappear for good (due to panic, accidents, or enemies) or they return home, kittens are the result.

- An unaltered male cat can father hundreds of kittens a year.

- Even if a person finds good homes for a litter of kittens, some of the kittens will grow up and produce litters of kittens.

- Spaying a female before her first heat protects her from risks of uterine, ovarian, and mammary cancers.

- Spaying also protects her from the stresses of pregnancy.

- Spaying reduces her frantic interest in the outdoors and reduces the chances that she'll wander far.

- Spaying reduces the chances she'll mark your home with urine when she's in heat.

- Un-neutered cats have urges that make them irritable and anxious. They yowl or whine frequently, fight with other cats, and/or destroy objects in the house.

- Neutering a male reduces his risk from numerous health problems.

- Neutering lowers his urge to roam and to fight, and thus lowers chances of disease transmission and woundings.

- Spaying and neutering helps dogs and cats live longer, healthier lives.

- Neutering makes pets less likely to roam the neighborhood or run away.

SOURCES: PetSmart Charities, Humane Society of the United States—Pet Overpopulation Facts (1999), Save Our Strays, Pet Savers Foundation, Spay USA, USA Today, June 23, 1998, p. 1, National Council of Pet Population Study and Policy—Shelter Statistics Survey (1997 data), The State of the American Pet—A Study Among Pet Owners, Prepared by Yahkelovich Partners for Ralston Purina, October, 2000. Journal of Applied Animal Welfare Science, 1998, Volume 1, Number 3, p. 213.

Spay/Neuter Organizations

Where You Can Be Part of the Solution

There are thousands of spay/neuter organizations at your fingertips. Just GOOGLE your area or call your local veterinarian, humane society or animal shelter and tell them you are looking for LOW-COST SPAY/NEUTER ASSISTANCE and...

The Animals Will Thank You!!

AC PAW—Grand Traverse Area Non—Profit Animal Rescue — AC PAW started as a vision of two people, Brian Manley and June McGrath, to ensure a safe haven for animals from abuse, hunger, disease and death. AC PAW was...
www.acpaw.org

The American Society for the Prevention of Cruelty of Animals (ASPCA) was the first humane society to be established in North America and is, today, one of the largest in the world. Our organization was founded by Henry Bergh in 1866 on the belief that animals are entitled to kind and respectful treatment at the hands of humans, and must be protected under the law...
www.aspca.org

Doris Day Animal Foundation...founded in 1978 as the Doris Day Pet Foundation by legendary performer, Doris Day, with a straightforward mission that continues to this day: to help animals and the people who love them...
www.dorisdayanimalfoundation.org

World Spay Day is an annual campaign of The HSUS and Humane Society International that shines a spotlight on spay/

neuter to save the lives of companion animals, feral cats, and street dogs who might otherwise be put down in a shelter or killed on the street. Start Planning Your World Spay Day 2014 Event!

www.humanesociety.org

The Humane Society of the United States is the nation's largest and most effective animal protection organization. We help animals by advocating for better laws to protect animals; conducting campaigns to reform industries; providing animal rescue and emergency response; investigating cases of animal cruelty; and caring for animals through our sanctuaries and wildlife rehabilitation centers, emergency shelters and clinics...

www.humanesociety.org

Morris Animal Foundation is a nonprofit organization that invests in science that advances veterinary medicine for companion animals, horses and wildlife. We are a global leader in animal health science, and our funding helps more species in more places than any other organization in the world.

www.morrisanimalfoundation.org

Spay USA—A nationwide network to provide affordable spay/neuter programs. Referrals, newsletter, articles, and advocacy. Call Spay/USA to get the names, phone numbers, and prices of services that have agreed to provide lower cost spay/neutering for cats and dogs in your local area. Private veterinarians, community programs, and special clinics participate nationwide. If your area needs additional spay/neuter services, request Spay/USA's packet of materials to distribute to local vets and organizations.

www.spayusa.org

Countless Animals Need Your Love. Help Heal Their Hearts. Enter your zip code and find info on local animal neutering.

www.localneutering.com

Spay and Neuter Solutions: Welcome!
www.spayandneutersolutions.org

SNAC: Spay/Neuter Alliance & Clinic is a 501(c)(3) non-profit organization that provides low-cost spays and neuters for cats and dogs. We provide free transport...
www.facebook.com/pages/SNAC-SpayNeuter...
Clinic/86524546841

Low Cost Spay/Neuter Organizations | Last Hope Animal Rescue
If you have a pet (cat or dog) that needs to be spayed or neutered and you are on disability, unemployed for 6 months or more, or on public assistance, LAST...
lasthopeanimalrescue.org

Spaying/Neutering—Caring for your pet—Through neutering, you can help your dog and cat live a happier, healthier, and longer... Having your pet spayed or neutered ensures that you will not be adding to this... American Humane Association is a 501(c)(3) non-profit organization.
www.americanhumane.org

Spay/Neuter Your Pet of Jackson County, Oregon—Jackson County, Oregon's only non-profit spay/neuter referral and assistance organization. The many ways SNYP helps...
www.spayneuter.org

MS-SPAN—Affordable Spay and Neuter!—MS-SPAN (Mississippi Spay And Neuter) is the first significant collaboration of non-profit animal welfare organizations from across the state of Mississippi.
www.msspan.org

Spay and Neuter Organizations and Resources—From Doris Day's "Spay Day USA" to lists of low-cost spay and neuter clinics, these resources will give you a head start toward understanding and taking a...
www.cats.about.com/od/resourcesandorganizations

Low-Cost Spay/Neuter Program Locator—PetSmart Charities
Statewide Agencies: Some organizations cover the entire state and are listed ... If you are a low-cost spay/neuter provider, or know

of one that is not in this...
www.petsmartcharities.org

Minnesota Spay Neuter Assistance Program—MN SNAP—There are other spay/neuter programs in Minnesota that are designed to help animal shelters and rescue organizations have their dogs and cats altered before...
www.mnsnap.org

You'll find here the best of all the "cat brags," along with the means to contribute your own cats' "show and tell," so jump right in to my cat lovers' community! Featured
www.cats.about.com

Orphans of the Storm | Links | Spay and Neuter Organizations Friends of Animals Assists in locating low cost spay/neuter providers in your area. 777 Post Road, Suite 205 Darien, CT 06820 1-800-321-PETS Ruth Helen Wolf Animal...
www.orphansofthestorm.org

Shenandoah Valley Spay and Neuter Clinic
www.spayandneuterclinic.org

The Purr-fect Cat Shelter (PCS) is a non-profit, no-kill, all-volunteer organization. It was established to provide temporary shelter and care for cats, with the ultimate goal of finding permanent homes for each cat. Cats accepted into the shelter stay as long as it is necessary. No cat will be destroyed because it has run out of time to find a home.
www.purrfectcatshelter.org

Low Cost Spay/Neuter Organizations | Last Hope Animal Rescue—Since 1981, Last Hope has been dedicated to the rescue and rehabilitation of stray, abandoned and death-due pound animals.
www.lasthopeanimalrescue.org

Spay/Neuter, Inc.—ABOUT US Founded in 1997 by concerned... Founded in 1997 by concerned local citizens, Spay/Neuter, Inc., is a

501c3, all volunteer, non-profit organization devoted to the welfare of dogs and cats in the...
www.spayneuterinc.org

Friends of Animals, Friends of Animals will send you an order form and a directory of participating veterinarians nationwide. You pay Friends of Animals for a certificate which you then take to the vet. Veterinarians are invited to call for information about participating.
www.friendsofanimals.org

North Shore Animal League, World's Largest NO-KILL Animal Rescue and Adoption Organization ... Our Mission: To build our hands-on rescue, rehabilitation and adoption efforts to save the lives of as many companion animals as possible—one at a time—and promote education to increase shelter adoptions, reduce animal cruelty and advance the highest standards in animal welfare ... Our Vision: Create a world where all companion animals find compassionate, permanent homes and to end animal cruelty and euthanasia.
www.animalleague.org

Mobile Spay & Neuter—Animal Rescue Coalition—ARC is a not-for-profit organization collaborating with local animal welfare organizations to end the killing of adoptable dogs and cats in Sarasota and Manatee...
www.animalrescuecoalition.org

Spay/Neuter Your Pet ... S.N.Y.P. is a non-profit organization dedicated to ending pet over-population. We are an all volunteer group that has joined together with Dallas-Ft. Worth humane groups and veterinarians to promote spaying or neutering of pets by providing reduced-price spay/neuter coupons. We do not have a shelter; all of our animals are kept in private foster homes. Looking for a reduced-price coupon to spay or neuter your pet in the Dallas-Ft. Worth area? Call us at 214-349-SNYP (7697) or send us your request with your...
www.dfwsnyp.com

Learn more: Top 10 Reasons to Spay or Neuter Your Pet ... If you are a low-cost spay/neuter provider, or know of one that is not in this database, ... at the ASPCA Adoptable Dogs in Your Local Shelter · Adoptable Cats in Your Local Shelter...

www.aspca.org/pet-care/spayneuter

Love That Cat—Programs that provide low cost or free spay/neuter for cats, listed by state. Some programs work only with pets of people with low incomes. Some do not consider income but serve only pet cats—or only feral (untame) cats. But other programs serve all kinds of people and cats. We believe the listing details below are correct at this writing, but call the program to be sure. If you know about other low cost or free spay/neuter programs or if you have updates to our listings, please contact us by clicking here...

www.lovethatcat.com

ASPCA Grants: Grants for Animal Shelters, Animal Control ... Grants for Animal Shelters, Animal Control, Non-sheltering Organizations and Spay/Neuter Programs

www.aspcapro.org

Spay/Neuter—« Pet Haven of Minnesota—Cat & Dog Rescue ... Why should I spay or neuter my pet? ... Organizations that participate in any of the following activities do not qualify for these grants: breeding animals; ...

www.pethavenmn.org

Spay Indiana | A program of the Humane Society of Indianapolis—For Organizations; Donate; Educational Resources and Printables; About. News; Contact; ... Follow us to learn about the latest spay/neuter news in Indiana!

www.spayindiana.org

Guide Star—Donors, grantmakers, and businesses can all benefit from GuideStar's nonprofit reports. Search our database of more than 1.8 million IRS-recognized nonprofit...

www.guidestar.org/organizations/20-0065631/spay-neuter-solutions.aspx

Sacramento Area Animal Coalition provides low-cost spay/neuter services through the following three programs: Voucher Program—operates year-round, helping low-income pet owners obtain spay/neuter surgeries at participating veterinary clinics for a small co-payment. Feral Cat Assistance Program provides low-cost spay/neuter surgeries for people who care for feral cat colonies. Spay Day is an annual event held in February for low-income pet owners.

www.sacanimal.org

Nongovernmental Organizations—Spay—Neuter Assistance Program—The Spay—Neuter Assistance Program works with various foundations and other animal welfare organizations to elevate the status of animals throughout the U.S. and in...

www.snapus.org

The place for pet adoption. Petfinder is the number one website for adoptable pets. Search over 350000 adoptable pets from nearly 14000 adoption groups.

www.petfinder.com

Meow.com—we here at Meow.com are very concerned about pet overpopulation. Every year hundreds of thousands of unwanted "pets" starve to death, are killed in accidents, or euthanized (killed) in shelters that cannot find homes for them. Meow.com supports spaying and neutering. We here at Meow.com are very concerned about pet overpopulation. Every year hundreds of thousands of unwanted "pets" starve to death, are killed in accidents, or euthanized (killed) in shelters that cannot find homes for them. Meow.com supports spaying and neutering. We see it as one of the most loving things you can do for your pet and for the animal world in general. For more information regarding spay and neuter, click on the link below. 10% of all profits for our "Fixed Cats" shirts shown above go to organizations who promote spaying and neutering. 25% of the selling price of our HOBO Strays goes to No-Kill Shelters. Give a cat gift that helps cats and sends an important message to all!

www.meow.com

Find Spay And Neuters at Great Prices.
www.Pronto.com

Animal Concerns Community—Spay and Neuter—Spay and Neuter—Organizations. Actions You Can Take (0) Articles (1) Educational Resources (2) E-Mail Lists (1) Events (0) General Info (0) Government Resources (0...

www.animalconcerns.org

Low-Cost Spay/Neuter Program Locator—PetSmart Charities | Statewide Agencies: Some organizations cover the entire state and are listed accordingly, ... If you are a low-cost spay/neuter provider,...

www.petsmartcharities.org/spay-neuter

Human Alliance—Spay/neuter is a simple solution to the complex problem of the euthanasia epidemic, ... and other animal welfare organizations in our community.

www.humanealliance.org

Organization—Feral Cat Spay/Neuter Project—The Feral Cat Spay/Neuter Project offers FREE spay/neuter ... collaborating with others and mentoring like-minded organizations to increase spay/neuter in...

www.volunteer.truist.com/uwkc/org

The Affordable Spay Neuter Clinic Home—We have performed thou-sands of spays and neuters since 1987 for rescue organizations and in private ... The Affordable Spay Neuter Clinic houses treatment ...

www.affordablespay.com

Targeted Spay/Neuter Program—PetSmart Charities—The Targeted Spay/Neuter grant offered by PetSmart Charities is intended to provide funding and mentoring ... Organizations are eligible to apply for only one of...

www.petsmartcharities.org

Washington animal organization receives grant for spay/neuter ... A Sultan, Wash. animal organization has much to celebrate for World Spay Day. Pasado's Safe Haven has received a grant from the Gary E. Milgard Family...

www.examiner.com

Humane Society—Tips and affording spay/neuter...
www.humanesociety.org/.../tips/afford_spay_neuter.html

ASPCA | Low-Cost Spay/Neuter Programs—Through our partnership with PetSmart Charities®, our comprehensive and searchable database is designed to help you find low-cost spay/neuter programs in your...
www.aspca.org

Low Cost Spay And Neuter ... Get The Biggest Bang For Your Buck. Explore Low Cost Spay And Neuter!
www.LocalSpaying.com

Spay/Neuter Grants ... Grant Money for Animal Spay Neuter Programs—For grant consideration, organizations must first submit a spay/neuter letter of inquiry including their federal tax identification number.
www.eHow.com/info_7750279_grant-animal-spay-neuter...

Each year VFHS awards grants to member organizations for spay/neuter services and programs in an effort to decrease intake in shelters across our state
www.vfhs.org

Spay and Neuter—Support Shelter and Rescue of Homeless Pets—Get a Cool T-Shirt AND donate to animal shelters and rescue organizations!
www.sheltershirts.webs.com

The Spay And Neuter Association Of Clatsop County in Astoria ... The Spay And Neuter Association Of Clatsop County: Employer Identification Number (EIN) 930852050: ... Organizations performing similar types of work: Id Name Address
www.nonprofitfacts.com/OR/The-Spay-And-Neuter-Association-Of...

Millan Foundation—What Is The Spay And Neuter Campaign? ... The Foundation has created a campaign that rescue organizations, veterinary clinics, spay/neuter programs,...
www.millanfoundation.org

Georgia Animal Project—Non-Profit Low-Cost Spay Neuter Clinics—individuals, reputable rescue organizations and animal shelters using highly skilled veterinarians, ... solution—high quality, low-cost spay and neuter clinics.
theanimalproject.org

Feral Cat Project—Save lives through prevention. Invest in Spay/Neuter. ... Individuals and organizations can help reduce the number of homeless cats by sponsoring a Feral Cat Spay/Neuter Project clinic.
www.feralcatproject.org

Petco Foundation—Events—National Spay and Neuter Drive— Pet overpopulation is one of the biggest problems facing companion animals and animal welfare organizations nationwide. Every year in the United States, 3–4 million...
www.petco.com/nsn

Local Organizations Support Humane Society of the United States 19th annual World Spay/Neuter Day on Feb. 26
www.businesswire.com/news/.../Local-Organizations-Support...

Spay and Neuter Solutions: Welcome!—Services: Spay and Neuter Solutions provides educational support and financial assistance to qualified owners for spaying and neutering their pets.
www.spayandneutersolutions.org

Ventura Thrift Store, SPAN Online—Join Our Mailing List! SPAN (Spay/Neuter Animal Network) is one of the MOST UNUSUAL NON-PROFIT organizations you will ever encounter.
www.spanonline.org

Spay/Neuter Your Pet of Jackson County, Oregon—Why Spay/ Neuter; Trap—Neuter—Return; Contact Us; Home; About SNYP; Get the Facts; Clients; Resources & Links; Volunteering; Help SNYP save lives ... organizations and...
www.spayneuter.org

Community Cats Spay/Neuter Funding: A Clarification—We are extremely grateful to Maddie's Fund for offering support for feral cat spay/neuter, ... as well as non-profit organizations (the ASPCA, The Toby Project,...

www.animalalliancenyc.org

Animal Protective Association of Missouri—Spay/Neuter Resources—At this time, the APA of Missouri does not offer spay and neuter services to the public. Below you will find a list of organizations that offer low-cost spay and...

www.apamo.org

Locate Affordable, Low Cost Spay/Neuter Resources—Low Cost or Free Spay and Neuter Resources in the USA and Worldwide searchable by state, province, country or area code

www.neuterspay.org

Pit Bull Rescue Central—To fund spay/neuter of owned pit bulls and pit bull mix programs: Ongoing, existing pit bull sterilization programs; ... Organizations may apply once per calendar year.

www.pbrc.net

ASPCA Grants : ASPCA Grants : ASPCA Professional—Grants for Animal Shelters, Animal Control, Non-sheltering Organizations and Spay/Neuter Programs. Guidelines and application instructions for spay/neuter programs,...

www.aspcapro.org

WHS Spay/Neuter Clinic :: Spay/Neuter Clinic :: Willamette ... —The NSNRT is a strategic training program which has helped more than 60 organizations open and operate spay/neuter clinics across the nation.

www.willamettehumanesociety.org

Holly Help Spay Neuter Fund—... we stand ready to refer pets with problems to those organizations and agencies that are being paid for their ... A sound spay-neuter program is the very...

www.hollyhelp.org

Spay and Neuter Shelter Scheduling—Social Responsibility— EZappt is happy to support our community through free use of our online service for designated non-profit organizations. We currently support spay and neuter clinics...

www.ezappt.com

Baton Rouge Spay/Neuter: About Us.—We also offer special contracts to humane organizations actively involved in spay/neuter. ... Baton Rouge Spay/Neuter a division of Spirit of Cheyenne

www.brsn.org

Spay & Neuter USA ... making a difference one pet at a time— Spay & Neuter has been established for 11 years · Supports various animal organizations · Seeking and supporting no surgical techniques for spaying and neutering

www.spayandneuterusa.com

Throughout February, World Spay Day events offer low-cost spay/neuter services for cats, dogs and other pets.

www.spaydayportal.humanesociety.org

Spay/Neuter and Wellness Clinic | Philadelphia Animal Welfare and rescue organizations that need affordable services to carry out their lifesaving work. ... PAWS Spay/Neuter and Wellness Clinic 2900 Grays Ferry Avenue

www.phillypaws.org/locations/spayneuter

Missouri Spay And Neuter Grants Now Available—JEFFERSON CITY, Mo.—The Missouri Department of Agriculture now has grants for 2013 available to animal shelters, rescue groups and other non-profit organizations...

www.ktts.com/news

Programs—Massachusetts Animal Coalition—Pit Bull Spay/ Neuter Task Force ... rescue groups and animal control organizations in Massachusetts by helping current Pit Bull owners keep their dogs happy, ..

www.massanimalcoalition.com

TDA Awards Spay/Neuter Grants to Tennessee Organizations—
MEMPHIS—The Tennessee Department of Agriculture today
announced the recipients of the animal spay/neuter grants at the
Mid-South Spay & Neuter Services in Memphis.
www.news.tn.gov

Spay/Neuter Programs—In-house/community spay and
neuter programs. These organizations provide low-cost spay and
neuter services, both in-house and assisting pet owners in their
communities.
www.kibblecanada.tripod.com

Spay/Neuter Myths | Animal Charity | Animal Organization ...
MYTH: It's better to have one litter before spaying a female pet.
FACT: Every litter counts. Medical evidence indicates just the
opposite. In fact, the evidence...
www.fixit—foundation.org

Spay San Diego FAQs—Spay San Diego—Who is performing
the spay/neuter surgeries and ... Since the groups or organizations
that are associated with Spay San Diego are offering their
services at...
www.spaysandiego.com

Spay/Neuter Services | The Humane Society of Tampa Bay—
Other Pet Organizations; Tampa Bay Dog Parks; Pet Loss & Grief;
Animal Health Center. Veterinary Services. ... Spay/Neuter Services
at the Animal Health Center.
www.humanesocietytampa.org

Washington Alliance for Humane Legislation—reduce the
burden on shelters, rescue organizations, ... How Spay/Neuter
Legislation Would Get the Job Done . Using a network of private,
public,...
www.savewashingtonpets.org

Helping to place loving pets in their forever homes—AFEW
has hosted a low cost spay/neuter van since 2003. ... professional

organizations. People for Animals Low Cost S/N Clinic 1 Sharon Road Robbinsville, NJ

www.afewpets.org

Animal Welfare | Ryan Newman Foundation—The Ryan Newman Foundation encourages families to adopt pets from animal shelters and pet rescue groups and to spay and neuter ... organizations across the...

www.ryannewmanfoundation.org

Low Cost Spay and Neutering Programs—Golden Retriever ... There are several national organizations that provide discounted spay and neuter certificates which can...

www.grrinews.org

Trap, Neuter, and Return Feral Cats—Volunteer Guide— Feral cats are a direct result of our failure to spay and neuter ... Neuter and Return programs are recommended by most animal organizations as the most humane and...

www.volunteerguide.org

Louisiana animal orgs offering low cost spay and neuter—New ... Check out www.spaynow.net for programs offering spay and neuter If cost is a factor in not having your pet spayed or neutered, animal organizations...

www.examiner.com

Why Spay or Neuter Your Pet? | The Sacramento Society for the ... Rescue Organizations; Other Area Shelters; Other Spay/Neuter Clinics; ... Spay/neuter decreases the homeless animal population. Shelters are full of homeless animals,...

www.sspca.org

News release :: Spay Montana—... no-cost spay and neuter surgeries to those in need in communities, ... it is a perfect match for the two organizations to merge,...

www.spaymontana.org

Part Three

◆

Animal Welfare Groups

Please Help Control the Pet Overpopulation.
Have Your Pet Spayed or Neutered!

Animal Welfare Groups

Where You Can Help

There are thousands of animal welfare groups at your fingertips. Just GOOGLE your area or call your local veterinarian, humane society or animal shelter and tell them...

YOU Want to Be PART of the SOLUTION!

The Animals Will Thank You!!

Animal welfare groups endorse the responsible use of animals to satisfy certain human needs. These range from companionship and sport, to many other uses.

Searches related to animal welfare groups include: Animal Welfare Groups List, Animal Rights Groups, International Animal Rights and Welfare Groups, Animal Cruelty Groups, ASPCA, American Humane Association, Animal Testing Groups.

Humane Society of the United States—The Humane Society of the United States is the nation's largest and most effective animal protection organization. We help animals by advocating for better laws to protect animals; conducting campaigns to reform industries; providing animal rescue and emergency response; investigating cases of animal cruelty; and caring for animals through our sanctuaries and wildlife rehabilitation centers, emergency shelters and clinics...
www.humanesociety.org

The American Society for the Prevention of Cruelty of Animals (ASPCA) was the first humane society to be established in North America and is, today, one of the largest in the world.

Our organization was founded by Henry Bergh in 1866 on the belief that animals are entitled to kind and respectful treatment at the hands of humans, and must be protected under the law...
www.aspca.org

Top Animal Welfare 2012 Nonprofit Organizations on ...
greatnonprofits.org/issues/animal—welfare—2012

Delaware Alliance for Animal Welfare Groups, Inc
www.daawgs.org

Organizations | Animal Welfare Information Center—Institute for Laboratory Animal Research (ILAR). National Academy of Sciences. Institute for Laboratory Animal Research. Develops and makes...
awic.nal.usda.gov/research-animals/organizations

Welcome to the Animal Behavior and Welfare Group at MSU!—Our Mission: The mission of the Animal Behavior and Welfare Group is to develop and to validate indicators of animal welfare and to effectively facilitate the use...
www.msu.edu/~zanella

Petfinder.com—Animal Welfare Organizations Near You—The virtual home of 313,064 adoptable pets from 13,724 adoption groups. Petfinder.com...
www.petfinder.com

Dec 13, 2012—Pet industry associations and animal welfare organizations have joined forces in an industry—wide effort to improve conditions for dogs and...
www.humanesociety.org/news/.../puppy-mills-coalition-121312. html

2 animal welfare groups pool efforts—Toledo Blade—PORT CLINTON—Two animal—welfare groups are working together to help each other and better serve the animals in their care.
www.toledoblade.com › News › Local

The Erie …—Animal Protection Organizations—Resources | THLN
   www.thln.org

Rodeo groups from across the country are uniting for the first time under the banner of the Australian Rodeo Federation … Grazier Craig Johnston on his property in West Wyalong, country NSW/Pic: Nathan Edwards Source: The Daily…
   NEWS.com.au by Simon Black

A Better World For Pets—See how Purina is helping pets in shelters all over the world.
   www.purina.com/PetWelfare

ASPCA Official Site—Helping Animals in Need—Support ASPCA Today. Support the Prevention of Cruelty to Animals.
   www.aspca.org/donate

Countless Animals Need Your Love. Help Heal Their Hearts. Animal Neutering Near You—Enter your zip code and find info on local anmal neutering.
   www.localneutering.com

Animal Health Foundation—Improving The Welfare of Animals
   www.animalhealthfoundation.net

HowStuffWorks "Animal Welfare Organizations"—Animal welfare organizations support the work that animal detectives provide. Learn how animal welfare organizations paved the road for detectives.
   www.science.howstuffworks.com/zoology/…animals/animal-detective1.htm

Animal welfare—OIE … Reports of ad hoc Groups on animal welfare are normally released to the public as annexes to reports of the Code Commission. The Code Commission meets in…
   www.oie.int/animal-welfare/animal-welfare-key-themes

Douglas Animal Welfare Group ... DAWG is a non-profit group of dedicated volunteers and members who rely entirely on donations, membership dues, grants, fund-raising events and recycling...
www.dawgrescue.com

Detroit Animal Welfare Group (DAWG)—Home
Detroit Animal Welfare Group (DAWG)—shelby twp., MI. A No Kill sanctuary for homeless animals.
www.dawghous.com

International Coalition for Animal Welfare (ICFAW)—Representing global animal welfare organizations at the OIE. ICFAW was formed in 2001 to represent non-governmental animal welfare organizations...
icfaw.org

UK animal welfare group unleashes drones to stop illegal hunting—RT ... Mar 17, 2013—In the UK, the latest drone surveillance technology will now be used by a leading animal welfare group to detect and catch illegal hunters...
rt.com/news/uk-drones-animals-hunting-374

Eurogroup For Animals ... Eurogroup for Animals is the leading voice for animal welfare at European Union level providing a voice for the billions of animals kept in laboratories, farms and...
eurogroupforanimals.org

Animal Health Foundation—Improving The Welfare of Animals
www.animalhealthfoundation.net

WSPA is working towards a world where animal welfare matters and animal cruelty ends. WSPA is the world's leading international alliance of animal welfare...
www.wspa-international.org

WSPA is a top animal rights charity working worldwide. Learn more.
wspa.thankyou4caring.org

Farm Animal Sanctuary—Join us in our fight to save farm animals from abuse and neglect.
www.woodstocksanctuary.org

Humane Society University—Animal control officers—share your stories of animal cruelty.
www.humanesocietyuniversity.or

Legal Rights for Animals—Help Protect The Rights Of Animals—Sign The ALDF Animal Bill Of Rights
org2.democracyinaction.org

Fixit Foundation—Our mission is to end overpopulation of companion animals by developing a system to support and promote incentive-based spay/neuter programs...
www.fixit-foundation.org

12,000 Cats & Dogs Die Every Day ... Help take spay/neuter to new levels ... Help Rescue Dogs & Cats
www.almosthomeanimals.org

Donate to 100% No-Kill Animal Shelter in Southfield, MI ... Help Stop Animal Abuse—AHA is leading the fight. Join us.
www.americanhumane.org/HelpAnimals

Nonhuman Rights Project—Working on legal rights for animals.
www.nonhumanrightsproject.org

*There are thousands of
animal welfare groups
at your fingertips.*

Pet Web Sites and Online Pet Stores

*Where You Can Help Simply with
the Click of Your Computer "Mouse"*

ASPCA (American Society for the Prevention of Cruelty to Animals), Animal Welfare Organizations, Animal Shelters, **www. PetFinder.com**, Charity USA*—including The Animal Welfare Rescue Site*, The Hunger Site*, The Breast Cancer Site*, The Veterans Site*, The Autism Site*, The Child Health Site*, The Literacy Site*, The Rainforest Site*, Greater Good Network Stores*, North Shore Animal League America, The Fund for Animals, National Wildlife Federation, International Fund for Animal Welfare, Rescue Bank—Helping People Helping Animals, The Center for Lost Pets, **www.bringfido.com**, pet friendly accommodations, parks, beaches, outdoor restaurants, off-leash parks, etc.

*****www.CharityUSA.com** is owner and operator of The Greater Good Network is an independent charitable organizations devoted to addressing the health and well-being of people, animals and the planet. The Greater Good Network websites bring together communities that care, giving people the power to make a difference in the world with simple, every day actions. The Greater Good Network websites include:

- The Animal Rescue Site funds food for abandoned animals in shelters and sanctuaries.

- The Hunger Site funds food for the world's hungry.

- The Breast Cancer Site funds mammograms for women in need.

- The Veterans Site funds meals for homeless and hungry veterans and their families.

- The Autism Site funds research and therapy to help children on the autism spectrum.

- The Child Health Site funds basic health services for children around the world.

- The Literacy Site funds new books for children in need.

- The Rainforest Site funds preservation of endangered rainforest habitat.

- Global Girlfriend helps women worldwide gain economic security.

- Greater Good Wholesale—shop where it matters.

- EcologyFund.com—protect and restore threatened ecosystems and wild habitats.

SOURCE: **www.greatergoodnetwork.com**

Part Four

◆

Feral Cats

70 Million and Counting

Please Help Control the Pet Overpopulation.
Have Your Pet Spayed or Neutered!

Feral Cats—70 million

Feral Cats and the Importance of Spaying/Neutering

It is estimated that there are 70 million feral and stray cats in the United States. A feral cat is defined as a cat born and raised in the wild, or who has been abandoned or lost and turned to wild ways in order to survive, is considered a free-roaming or feral cat. While some feral cats tolerate a bit of human contact, most are too fearful and wild to be handled. Feral cats often live in groups, called colonies, and take refuge wherever they can find food—rodents and other small animals and garbage. They will also try to seek out abandoned buildings or deserted cars—or even dig holes in the ground—to keep warm in winter months and cool during the summer heat.

SOURCE: **www.aspca.com**—ASPCA (American Society for the Prevention of Cruelty to Animals)

Links are provided in "Feral Cats and How You Can Help," which include animal welfare organizations, spay/neuter assistance programs and organizations that specialize in feral cats and their colonies.

Searches related to Feral Cats include: Feral Cat Organizations, Feral Cats, Feral Cat Traps, Feral Cat Rescue

It is estimated that
there are 70 million feral and stray cats
in the United States.

Feral Cats and How You Can Help

Feral Cat Organizations

Feral cats are the forgotten felines—the throwaways and castoffs of uncaring humans.

Feral Cats are defined as a cat born and raised in the wild, or who has been abandoned or lost and turned to wild ways in order to survive, is considered a free—roaming or feral cat (see "Feral Cats—70 Million" for more info.). Cat lovers as well as bird lovers will want to help these creatures. Listed below are just a few of the thousands of web sites. Just GOOGLE "FERAL CAT ORGANIZATIONS" in your area or call your local veterinarian, humane society or animal shelter and tell them you are looking for assistance with FERAL cats so...

YOU Can Be PART of the SOLUTION!

The Cats (and the Birds) Will Thank You!!

You can improve the lives of outdoor cats with Trap—Neuter—Return, the humane and effective approach for feral cats. To successfully trap, neuter, vaccinate, eartip, and return feral cats, you need a plan. These guidelines for humane trapping from Alley Cat Allies, the organization that is dedicated to protecting and improving the lives of our nation's cats, advocating trap/neuter/return as a method of reducing feral cat populations.
www.alleycat.org

"The Vacuum Effect: Why Catch and Kill Doesn't Work—Removing cats from an area by killing or relocating them is not only cruel—it's pointless. Scientific research, years of failed attempts, and evidence from animal control personnel prove the vacuum effect and that catch and kill doesn't permanently clear an area of cats. Feral Cats and the Public—A Healthy Relationship: The science behind why feral cats are safe members of our communities—Public health policies all over the country reflect the scientific evidence: feral cats live healthy lives outdoors and don't spread disease to people." **www.alleycat.org**

These rescue groups find abandoned cats, vaccinate and neuter them,...

Search for **Feral Cat Organizations** Look Up Fast Results now! **www.ask.com/Feral+Cat+Organizations**

Search for **Feral Cat Rescue Groups** w/100's of Results at WebCrawler
www.cat.webcrawler.com

Find groups that help feral cats in the U.S. using our map.
What You Can Do to Help Feral Cats: The Humane Society of the ... If you're really lucky, there is an organization or agency in your community that can help you trap-neuter-return the feral cats you're feeding. If this help isn't...
www.humanesociety.org

ASPCA | Feral Cats FAQ
While some feral cats tolerate a bit of human contact, most are too fearful and wild to be handled. Ferals often live in groups, called colonies, and take refuge...
www.aspca.org

Castaway Critters—Our mission is to save and nurture homeless dogs and cats to match companion animals with loving, life-long homes, to foster responsible pet care, to control overpopulation in our community thru spay/neuter programs and...
www.castawaycritters.org

Alley Cat Allies—Dedicated to protecting and improving the lives of our nation's cats. Organization advocating trap/neuter/return as a method of reducing feral cat populations. Alley Cat Allies, is the national nonprofit clearinghouse for information on feral and stray cats. For more than a decade Alley Cat Allies has advocated Trap-Neuter-Return (TNR)—the most humane and effective method to reduce feral cat populations.

www.alleycat.org

Feral Cat Coaltion—in response to the staggering problem of feral (wild) cat problems, The FCC is an organization that live traps...

www.feralcat.com

Paws For The Cause Feral Cat Rescue—We focus on feral (wild) cats and adoptions of kittens or animals rescued from...

www.pawsforthecauseferalcatrescue.org

Metro Ferals —An all-volunteer organization established to reduce the suffering of feral cats and kittens by promoting a non-lethal alternative to the feral cat population ... DC metro feral cat organization, donate save cats, feral...

www.metroferals.org

Rescue Groups—Feral Cats
www.cats.about.com/od/feralrescue

Feral cats remain a hot-button issue—Minneapolis Star Tribune—The explosive issue of free-roaming cats—feral and domesticated—and their ... by some groups as an alternative to euthanizing feral cats. ? Catch and release? Minneapolis rethinks stray cat approach—Article by: BRIAN AROLA , Star Tribune Updated: March 7, 2013—11:56 PM ... City Council Member Cam Gordon wants to scrap the catch and euthanize program in favor of a trap, neuter- or spay-and-release approach, similar to what St. Paul does, saying it is more humane and effective in controlling the stray cat population.

www.startribune.com/sports/outdoors/200735561.html

Feral Cats—Merrimack River Feline Rescue Society—The MRFRS got its start as a feral cat organization. While the feral cat problem in Newburyport and surrounding areas is largely under control,...

www.mrfrs.org/feral-cats

Feral Cat Assistance Program—Greensboro...
www.petfinder.com/shelters

Feral Cats: The Humane Society of the United States—Feral and stray cats are the most significant source of cat overpopulation. We'll help you help them. Read more...
www.humanesociety.org/issues/feral_cats

Former Covington resident bequeaths $400,000 to ...—New Orleans—The heft donation relieves the organization of its fundraising duties so it can concentrate on its primary mission, to spay and neuter feral cats...
www.nola.com/pets

Feral cat organizations and bird lovers to face off at Cook County ... The cat verses bird debate will take center stage at the Cook County Commissioners meeting on Tuesday. The spotlight will shine on the ...
www.examiner.com

Stanford Cat Network | Links and Resources for Feral Cat Care ...
catnet.stanford.edu

KittiCo Cat Rescue: A Non-Profit No-Kill 501(c)(3) Organization ... This is the home page for KittiCo Cat Rescue: An all volunteer 501(c)(3) no-kill organization dedicated to the rescue and care of stray and feral cats in Dallas,...
www.kittico.org

Feral Cat Trap—Neuter—Return Program | Austin Humane Society—But left unchecked, these stray cats will cause a population boom that won't be good for them or us. So we're happy to be the only organization in Austin offering...
www.austinhumanesociety.org

Feral Cats Program | The Humane Society of Tampa Bay— While some feral cats tolerate a bit of human contact, most are not socialized to people. Feral cats typically live in groups called colonies and have strong social...
humanesocietytampa.org/feralcats

Maddie's Fund—New York City Feral Cat Council—Bryan Kortis serves as chair of the New York City Feral Cat Council (NYCFCC), a coalition of twelve feral cat organizations that utilize Trap-Neuter-Return (TNR)...
www.maddiesfund.org

Maddie's Fund—How to Start a Feral Cat Program—Organizations on even the smallest budget can start a feral cat program. It's as simple as starting a feral cat caregiver support group, offering free spay/neuter to...
www.maddiesfund.org

Feral Cat Program—Reno—Community Cats is a non-profit organization dedicated to the reduction of feral cat overpopulation through sterilization, the improvement of feral cats' quality of...
www.washoecounty.us

The Humane Society of the United States—Here is a comprehensive list of feral cat-related organizations, listed alphabetically by state.
www.humanesociety.org

Feral Feline Organization—Davis Wiki—The Feral Feline Organization (FFO) is a community non-profit group in Davis. We are dedicated to helping the lives of feral cats. As you have most likely seen,...
daviswiki.org/Feral_Feline_Organization

Feral Cat Organizations in Texas—cats, Panther City Feral Cat ... Feral cat organizations in Texas. Aggie Feral Cat Alliance of Texas College Station www.cvm.tamu.edu/afcat. Austin Feral Cats Austin www.austinferalcats.org...
www.fortworthferals.org/feralcatorganizationsintexas.html

Trap, Neuter, Return Program—Dallas Animal Services—This means a program approved by the director in which feral cats are humanely ... DAS personnel assisted by feral cat groups will be available to address any...
www.dallasanimalservices.org/trap_neuter_return.html

*Feral cats are
the forgotten felines—
the throwaways and castoffs
of uncaring humans.*

How YOU can safely rescue...

One Animal at a Time!

Any time, any place, you may encounter an animal that needs your help!

Always remember whenever, wherever you are helping an animal, RESPECT, RESPECT, RESPECT! Them AND You! Even when we are trying to help an animal in distress, keep in mind that they don't always know that and although they will sense your good intentions, they are still scared, possibly hungry and **FOR SURE TRAUMATIZED**!! You want to always be safe as well as keeping the animal protected and free from any more harm than has already happened to him/her.

The first step in rescuing is to assess the situation and conditions. Watch for traffic, other animals, people, anything that could put you in harm's way.

NEVER let children rescue and I strongly recommend that they are kept away from the rescuing scene as there are many things that can happen and possibly endanger them as well as the adult rescuer.

Let the rescued animal adjust slowly, keeping them in their live trap so as to not expose other pets you may have to disease, biting or stress. A trip to the veterinarian is required immediately to assure good health for the rescued pet, you and other pets. You may have to contact a rescue group as well if unable to keep the rescued pet. I never try to rescue a wild animal. If necessary, call your local veterinarian to see who should be contacted. Remember, a wild animal is just that, a wild animal. So no matter how "cute" they are, they are still wild and belong in the wild. Many people try to adopt wild animals, including raccoons, only to find they bite, chew, attack and are not a good fit to be living with humans. Let's enjoy wild animals in the wild, not in our homes! Animals truly are awesome in the right setting!

Any time, any place,
you may encounter an animal
that needs your help!

Part Five

◆

Pet Friendly Accommodations

Please Help Control the Pet Overpopulation.
Have Your Pet Spayed or Neutered!

Pets Welcome Here!

Pet Friendly Accomodations—
Complete with Links and Phone Numbers

In addition to the 72.9 million U.S. households who own a pet, there are 60,000 pet friendly hotels, including well-known names of hotel chains such as:

Affinia Hotels – **www.affinia.com** – 866-246-2203

Aloft – **www.starwoodhotels.com** – 877-GO-ALOFT

America's Best Value Inn – **www.americasbestvalueinn.com** – 888-315-2378

Americinn – **www.americinn.com** – 800-634-3444

Ascend Collection – **www.ascendcollection.com** – 877-424-6423

Baymont – **www.baymontinns.com** – 888-426-0295

Best Western – **www.bestwestern.com** – 800-780-7234

Candlewood Suites – **www.candlewoodsuites.com** – 800-439-4745

Clarion – **www.clarionhotel.com** – 877-424-6423

Comfort Inn – **www.comfortinn.com** – 877-424-6423

Comfort Suites – **www.comfortsuites.com** – 877-424-6423

Country Inn and Suites by Carlson – **www.countryinns.com** – 800-830-5222

Courtyard by Marriott – **www.marriott.com** – 866-235-8098

Crowne Plaza – **www.crowneplaza.com** – 800-439-4745

Days Inn – **www.daysinn.com** – 800-682-1082

Delta – **www.deltahotels.com** – 888-890-3222

Doubletree – **www.doubletree.hilton.com** – 888-370-0998

Drury Hotels – **www.druryhotels.com** – 800-378-7946

Econolodge – **www.econolodge.com** – 877-424-6423

Embassy Suites – **www.embassysuites.hilton.com** – 888-370-0985

Extended Stay – **www.extendedstaysamerica.com** – 800-804-3724

Fairfield Inn & Suites – **www.marriott.com/fairfield.com** – 888-236-2427

Four Points by Sheraton – **www.fourpoints.com** – 800-368-7764

Guesthouse Inn – **www.guesthouseinnhotels.roomstays.com** – 866-235-8098

Hampton Inn – **www.hamptoninn.hilton.com** – 888-370-0981

Hawthorn Suites – **www.hawthorn.com** – 888-215-2756

Hilton Garden Inn – **www.hiltongardeninn.com** – 888-370-0984

Hilton Hotel – **www.hiltonhotel.com** – 800-774-1500

Holiday Inn – **www.holidayinn.com** – 800-439-4745

Holiday Inn Express – **www.ihg.com/holidayinnexpress** – 800-439-4745

Homewood Suites – **www.homewoodsuites.hilton.com** – 888-370-0983

Hotel Indigo – **www.hotelindigo.com** – 877-846-3446

Howard Johnson – **www.hojo.com** – 800-741-5072

Hyatt – **www.hyatt.com** – 888-553-1300

Intercontinental – **www.intercontinental.com** – 800-439-4745

Jameson Inn – **www.jamesoninns.com** – 800-526-3766

Kimpton – **www.kimptonhotels.com** – 800-546-7866

Knights Inn – **www.knightsinn.com** – 866-365-9867

La Quinta – **www.lq.com** – 800-753-3757

Loews – **www.loewshotels.com** – 800-235-6397

Mainstay – **www.mainstaysuites.com** – 877-424-6423

Marriott Hotel – **www.marriot.com** – 877-976-0576

Microtel Inn & Suites – **www.microtelinn.com** – 800-337-0050

Motel 6 – **www.motel6.com** – 800-466-8356

Omni – **www.omnihotels.com** – 800-843-6664

Quality – **www.qualityinn.com** – 877-424-6423

Radisson – **www.radisson.com** – 800-967-9033

Ramada – **www.ramada.com** – 800-851-2344

Red Lion – **www.redlion.com** – 855-261-1568

Red Roof Inn – **www.redroof.com** – 800-733-7663

Renaissance – **www.marriott.com** – 877-976-0576

Residence Inn by Marriott – **www.marriott.com** – 877-976-0576

Rodeway – **www.rodewayinn.com** – 877-424-6423

Sheraton – **www.sheraton.starwoodhotels.com** – 800-325-3535

Sleep Inn – **www.sleepinn.com** – 877-424-6423

Springhill Suites – **www.marriott.com** – 877-976-0576

Staybridge Suites – **www.staybridge.com** – 877-238-8889

Studio 6 – **www.staystudio6.com** – 888-897-0202

Suburban – **www.suburbanhotels.com** – 877-424-6423

Super 8 – **www.super8.com** – 800-536-0719

Towneplace Suites – **www.marriott.com** – 877-976-0576

Travelodge – **www.travelodge.com** – 800-525-4055

Westin – **www.westinstarwoodhotels.com** – 800-937-8461

Wingate by Wyndham – **www.wyndham.com** – 888-215-2756

SOURCE: www.tripswithpets.com

Bringfido.com

Bringfido.com is a dog travel directory that provides unbiased reviews, detailed pet policy information and on-line reservations at more than 25,000 pet friendly hotels and Bringfido.com has a partnership with Travelocity. There are 60,000 pet friendly accommodations in the U.S.

Information is also available on thousands of bed & breakfasts, vacation rentals and campgrounds that welcome pets in 150 countries.

When making vacation plans, dog owners look to Bringfido.com for the lowdown on both airlines and hotel pet policies, as well as recommendations on dog beaches, off-leash parks, outdoor restaurants and other animal attractions in more than 10,000 cities around the world. **Bringfido.com** has a toll-free number (877-411-FIDO) dog owners can call if they need assistance locating a pet friendly hotel at the next exit on the highway, an animal hospital that is open at 4 a.m. or the best restaurant in Little Italy that allows dogs to sit at its outdoor tables.

Since launching in April, 2005, **Bringfido.com** has helped more than half a million people take their dog on vacation. When you are looking for somewhere to stay, play or eat with your dog, Bringfido.com is the place to come.

This does not include the almost 4,000 pet friendly campgrounds in the U.S. **Bringfido.com** is a web site dedicated to traveling with your pet and includes the following informational links which detail the number of accommodations, attractions and pet services in the U.S.

Accommodations listed on **www.Bringfido.com**

Hotels & Motels—19, 391; Bed & Breakfasts—823; Vacation Rentals—10,244; Long-term Apartments—70, Campgrounds—3,969.

SOURCE: www.Bringfido.com

Pet Attractions listed on **www.Bringfido.com**

Dog Parks—2,570; Dog Beaches—290; Dog Friendly Hiking Trails—6,008; Dog Friendly Tours—133; Pet Friendly Shopping—195; Other Attractions—451.

Pet Services listed on **www.Bringfido.com**

Pet Sitting and Dog Walking—2,551; On-line Resources—191; Dog Training—1,506; Dog Grooming—1,323; Pet Stores—2,039; Dog Boarding Kennels—669; Other Pet Services—512.

SOURCE: www.Bringfido.com

Pets Welcome Here!

*In addition to the 72.9 million
U.S. households who own a pet,
there are 60,000 pet friendly hotels,
including well-known names
of hotel chains.*

Traveling with Your Four-Legged Friend

Can Be Fun and Enjoyable if You Plan Carefully!

A family vacation is just that, a "family" vacation, which includes taking your four-legged family members with you. People do travel with their cats. However, this article will focus on traveling with your cruisin' canine friend. Here are some ideas to help you prepare for your adventure when traveling by car, relaxing at your favorite hotel or bed & breakfast, or sitting in front of a glowing campfire with your best friend.

Preparing to Travel

Before making travel plans, ask yourself if your dog is able to travel. An older dog may have trouble laying/sitting for long periods of time. A puppy may require frequent "potty" breaks. Check with your veterinarian for an assessment. If you get your vet's approval, but your dog is not accustomed to long trips, try a short overnight or weekend trip first.

Make an appointment with your veterinarian and inform him of your travel plans. Make certain that your dog is up to date on all vaccinations and obtain their current health and rabies certificates to take along with you. In the event of a medical emergency, having your dog's medical history will expedite medical care and reduce the potential of duplicating vaccinations.

Knowing where veterinarians are along your route and at your destination is a good idea. **www.healthypet.com** has a trip planner that lets you enter your route into MapQuest and then shows where accredited pet hospitals are along the way.

Your dog should always wear a secure collar complete with rabies vaccination tags and license and you should have a tag with your contact information on it. You can also use a permanent marker and write your name, address, phone number, and your dog's name on the inside of the collar. Keep an extra copy of your dog's tag numbers, rabies certificate, and license information and carry it in your wallet.

Even if your dog has a collar, when dogs become separated from their owners, oftentimes they come back without a collar. You should strongly consider having your dog micro chipped. You also may want to consider placing a flashing red light on your dog's collar at night time.

Once you've done that, here are a few things you will want to remember to bring along.

1. Water and Bowls (make sure your dog has fresh water at all times)
2. Dog Food and Treats (avoid sudden changes of diet)
3. List of veterinary hospitals near the location where you are staying
4. Collar with tags
5. Sturdy leash (not longer than six feet)
6. Crate or kennel and dog bed
7. One or two toys
8. Pooper scooper and paper towels
9. Bags to pick up doggie do
10. Your dog's medical records
11. Sheets to cover bedding and furniture at your destination
12. Recent picture of your dog that includes name, breed, sex, age, microchip or tattoo numbers, description including coat, color, weight, height, markings, scars, other identifying marks.

A few more thoughts: Have your dog's nails clipped. Freshly trimmed nails are less likely to cause property damage and your dog will be easier to restrain if necessary. Don't let your dog ride with his head hanging out, as this can cause eye injuries. Restrain your dog using a dog seat belt or crate.

Car Travel

A crate is an excellent way to keep your dog safe in the car. If staying in a hotel, keeping your dog in his crate while you are out shopping can keep your dog safe and out of trouble. Make sure your dog is accustomed to a crate before traveling. Once your dog is ready for his big adventure, make sure his crate is sturdy, properly ventilated, and of adequate size so he can stand up in, turn around, and lie down comfortably. The bottom should be leak proof and covered with towel or dog's bedding. Put your dog's favorite toy and a water bottle (secured properly) inside the crate. The crate should have strong carrying handles and never leave a leash inside the crate as your dog could get tangled in it. If your dog is not accustomed to car trips, start out with short rides. Starting out with an empty tummy will help avoid carsickness. Make sure your dog has plenty of water. Keep your car well ventilated and when your dog is crated make sure fresh air can flow into the crate at all times.

Car rides can be boring; playing the radio and talking to your dog may be soothing.

Never, ever, leave your dog unattended in a closed vehicle, or with the window down just a little, even for five minutes. Have a family member stay with your dog. Even on a cloudy, "cool" day, the temperature in a car can rise to life-threatening temperatures, even if parked in the shade as shade moves. Remember, your dog's body temperature is higher than humans. Leaving your dog in an unattended vehicle also increases the chances for dog theft. And as cute as your dog may be, people love petting a dog, even if they are "protecting" their owner's car. Leaving your dog alone in the car creates a risk for your dog and any animal lovers wanting to give your dog a little pat.

Stop frequently for exercise and potty breaks. Take breaks just as you do at home with your dog and maybe even a little more frequently on a trip as the dog may be experiencing a little more stress (and excitement) than while at home. Be sure to clean up after your dog. When taking breaks, never let your dog run loose.

Your New Home Away from Home

A little dog owner etiquette goes a long way with fellow guests and the proprietor. Keep your dog as quiet as possible. Put your dog's toys, water, and food bowls out for them immediately so your dog will feel more "at home".

Bring in your dog's crate with his bedding. If you absolutely have to leave your dog in the room alone, leave your dog in his crate. Leave the TV or radio on for your dog. Let the front desk know you will be leaving your dog crated in your room and to call you immediately if there is a problem and you will return immediately.

Ask the management where you are allowed to walk your dog and be sure to use your pooper-scooper. Wipe your dog's paws before returning to your lodging. Cover furniture and beds and never allow your dogs to sleep on beds or chairs. When checking out, leave your room clean and free of dog hair. Taking a little hand-held vacuum is always a good idea too!

If you choose to take your best friend camping, make sure the campground is dog friendly. Some campgrounds have pet free camping areas. Some campground web sites state that pets are welcome in state parks, recreation areas and at boating access sites, but they must be accompanied at all times by responsible owners.

Most national parks allow for dogs. Check each individual park web site for more information and rules.

Happy traveling!

Part Six

◆

How to Be a Responsible Pet Owner

Please Help Control the Pet Overpopulation.
Have Your Pet Spayed or Neutered!

Pet Adoption

How to Be a Responsible Pet Owner

YOU can help, one animal at a time and for THAT animal, you have made a world and lifetime of difference.

Adopting a cat, kitten or dog from an animal shelter makes YOU a life saver and for MORE than ONE animal. Adopting from an animal shelter makes room for another homeless animal, keeping that animal from being euthanized and allows for other animals awaiting their forever home, more time to stay at the shelter and be united with their new owner. By rescuing from a no-kill pet rescue organization, you're allowing that organization to rescue another pet from a public shelter, which, of course, saves the life of that pet plus the lives of other pets at that shelter by creating space so other animals can be kept longer. As you can see, adoption is truly a continuous cycle of saving lives!

Think and plan about the pet you will adopt. If you like cute and cuddly while being in a position to "potty train" a puppy, maybe adopting a "youngster" is the animal for you. When adopting a cat/kitten, personality is something to consider, although be aware that in a shelter setting, an animal may be less outgoing and a little reserved or even frightened. Bringing a critter home will bring out the best of them. A rambunctious puppy in a shelter setting will soon become accustomed to your and his/her new home once they are settled into a routine and their new found forever home. Whether adopting a dog or a cat, puppy or kitten, have a good idea about what kind of personality you want your new adopted pet to have. What is your lifestyle like? Do you already have a pet at home? A dog, cat, kids and what ages are they. When you adopt an adult from a rescue or animal shelter instead of buying a kitten from a pet shop, what you see is what you get. Their personality is already mostly developed, and you'll be able to spot the characteristics you're looking for much more easily than with a kitten bought at a store or from a breeder looking to make a buck.

Rescue organizations, and many shelters that provide pet adoption counseling, are able to assess the personality of each pet for adoption, and carefully match you up with the right pet for your lifestyle. With a kitten, of course, there is a lot more guesswork involved. Want to adopt a cat who will instantly fit in with your family? That's easy when you adopt an adult from a kitten rescue organization or shelter!

As our society gets older, oftentimes, a person who has owned a pet and is no longer able to care for that pet, is looking for a good home for their pet. Sometimes, family members take over this responsibility. This may mean acquiring an older dog. While you may not get the number of years from this animal as if you had adopted them as a puppy or kitten, they are potty trained, socialized and just looking for love! Keep in mind they may be grieving the loss of their original owner. Just give them extra hugs and more love and they will adjust to their new home.

Animals of all ages can be found for adoption. And please remember, they cannot tell us where it hurts, so keep a close eye on the health of your pet and get regular medical check ups—just like with us humans!

Cat & kitten adoption equals an instant friend for life. Ask anyone who has adopted a cat or kitten, and they'll swear their bond is deep and pure. We all want to be loved and that is certainly true with animals. Some like to be hugged more than others. Some like to snuggle for naps, some like to sleep all day and rip and tear at night. When you open your heart and your home to a pet who needs help, they really do show their appreciation for the rest of their life! Cats who have been uprooted from their homes, or have had difficult beginnings are likely to bond completely and deeply with their new human caretakers. No matter who or what you adopt, your newfound critter friend will consider you a hero. After all, you have rescued them from a cage and sometimes abuse they have experienced before coming to the shelter or rescue group. Kitties who find themselves in the shelter or at a rescue because of a death or other tragedy in their former human family usually go through a mourning period.

Once they are adopted, however, they usually want nothing more than to please their new hero—YOU!

No matter what circumstances brought them to the rescue, most cats and kittens for adoption are exceptionally affectionate and attentive, and make wonderful companions. But first you have to adopt one!

Once you have adopted, you will continue to adopt and wonder how you ever lived without your new lifelong companion!

Always have fresh water for your pet. Check with your veterinarian when deciding what to feed your new best forever friend. Age, weight and health are all factors that vary depending upon the animal. When taking them in the car with you, NEVER, EVER!!! leave your pet in a hot car. Sometimes that may not be easy to tell what is "hot". For us humans, we can tolerate heat better than an animal as their body temperature is higher than ours. In a car, with the sun shining in through the windows, you get a greenhouse effect and even on a cloudy, 60 degree day, the temperature can rise to dangerous conditions for your pet. Even leaving the window "cracked" is not safe for your pet. Leaving the window down too far, is dangerous for your pet as he/she may jump out or someone could reach in to pet your animal friend and that is risky business as even the most docile pet is "protecting" their owner's car and may snap or bite. The animal could also get stolen, even a big breed. So if in doubt, leave your pet at home and don't forget to throw the tennis ball for him/her when you get home and ALWAYS give your pet a humongous hug as they welcome you like you've been gone for years!

Get the required vaccinations at the scheduled time. Have the name and number of your vet posted where you can find it quickly. NEVER let your cat be outside without supervision. There are many predators out there, from hawks to coyotes and your newfound friend could be swept away in a minute. Cars, bikes, chemicals left out by neighbors while working on their vehicles, or spraying their lawns can be hazardous to your pet. I am careful when I walk so I don't track in anything that could harm my pet. When cleaning my home, I check with my vet before using cleaners, including floor cleaners. Remember, pets will lick their paws—dogs and cats and even a minute amount of a "chemical" can kill your pet. NEVER, EVER, give your pet anything by mouth except as allowed by your vet, including "over the counter" type medicine. If in doubt, a quick phone call to your vet will give you peace of mind and keep your pet safe. And always,

PLEASE HELP CONTROL THE PET OVERPOPULATION!

HAVE YOUR PET SPAYED OR NEUTERED!

After you bring your friend home, the shelter or rescue group is a great source of knowledge. They can be there during your pet's transition. When adopting from a shelter or rescue group, you're adopting a healthier pet! Nearly all public shelters and rescues spay or neuter their pets for adoption and administer all necessary vaccines before they allow you to take your new pet home. They want to make sure your kitty has at least nine lives and your puppy usually comes with a "puppy guide", especially made for new owners. If the animal has not already been fixed, a spay/neuter fee is usually required and after your pet is "fixed", you will usually get a portion of this fee returned to you.

If an animal has been placed in a foster home, they may already be potty trained or litter box trained. Keep in mind however, they will have to adjust to their new home with you. Keeping the litter box clean and smelling nice is more inviting to your new friend. A puppy will require more attention to training than a cat/kitten. Potty breaks are required, during good and bad weather. So get your boots, jacket or sunscreen, as your puppy will have to "go" often until trained and he is mature enough to be able to "hold it".

If you have other pets, introduce them slowly. Never force them to get along. They will in time. Make sure everyone has their own space, including food and water bowls. The sweetest, kindest animals may squabble over food, even if you have 20 pounds of it in front of them. That is just human or should I say animal nature.

When introducing your pet to children, depending upon the age, I always keep my pet's food away from the kids, especially if they are very young. However, snapping or aggression of any kind should never be tolerated and with a little time, patience and training, it is most likely everyone will get along. NEVER allow kids to tease an animal with ANYTHING, including sticks, blowing in the animal's face, etc.

While some people may not agree, I believe in "crating" my newfound dog/puppy. This is far better than coming home to a destroyed home, which not only creates anger in you, the owner, but the animal knows they have done wrong too, but simply cannot help themselves. Puppies teeth and they chew. It can be hazardous to their health. I have seen chewed remote controls, including the batteries, plastic, furniture, shoes, anything in a typical home. When I mentioned to the pet owners to crate their pet, they thought it was cruel. It is NOT cruel to crate your dog with the proper crate, including enough space and water, toys, etc. It is even better if a neighbor or friend can assist with letting the dog/puppy out for breaks when you are away.

Check for obedience classes and behavioral classes in your area. For dog owners, they are fun and you and your friend will meet new people, two-legged and four-legged. For assistance with any problems you may experience if adopting a fabulous feline, ask your veterinarian.

Please be aware of the risks of buying from a pet store, puppy mill or "backyard" breeder. When buying from a "pet store", they are usually getting their animals from one of two sources: 1) a "backyard" breeder, or 2) a /puppy/kitten mill. The majority of purebred animals in shelters or rescues are the product of "backyard" breeders who often sell puppies/kittens through the newspaper classified ads. These are people who think they can make some easy money by breeding their purebred dogs and cats and then making their money back by selling them. Some people think that because they have a "purebred" dog they can breed with another "purebred" dog. They have no clue what they are doing and they don't think about the repercussions of bringing yet a "few more" animals into the world. Many of the kittens/puppies are weaned from their mothers way too soon, have not gotten their shots, may be feline leukemia positive and of course, the "breeder" is not aware of this and usually does not care. I have heard people refer to their "barn cats" as "good mousers". This is not only unhealthy for the pet, but the recipient of the pet as well. These "mousers" will have worms and other health problems, may be feline leukemia positive and usually live off the land, as opposed to eating healthy dog or cat food.

Puppy mills and kitten mills are just that, mills where cats and dogs are bred as often as possible, fed the worst possible food at best, kept in cages you would not keep a maggot in and made to "live" in unsanitary conditions with little human contact. While this book is all-age friendly, I suggest you GOOGLE puppy or kitten mills for more information. If you know of a puppy or kitten mill, PLEASE report this to the nearest animal shelter, humane society or your veterinarian. You can help the abused animals and close the puppy/kitten mills!

NEVER BUY A KITTEN, CAT, DOG OR PUPPY FROM A PET STORE! Even some well-known pet store chains get their animals from a puppy/kitten mill. Check them out first. Even a clean store front does not reveal what goes on behind closed doors!

Check your classified ads too for puppies/kittens. These animals will usually be thrown from cars, dumped in boxes on the side of the road, taken to the woods for execution or sold to research labs. And while you are talking to the pet owners who have a "FREE" puppy, kitten, please tell them to get their pet spayed or neutered and point them in the right direction. REMEMBER— one animal at a time makes a lifetime of a difference for that particular animal.

Remember, adoption is the most humane option!

Respect your pet and your pet will respect you. Animals offer us unconditional love. They are always there for us. They ask for nothing and they get us through things that some humans could never get us through. And they're cheaper than therapy.

It is a good idea to have an "emergency" contact on your phone who will be called to take care of your pets in the event you cannot get home due to an emergency. Make sure that person is just as responsible as you are and in the event of the need to find homes for your critter friends, find a friend who is willing to take on that duty.

Again, animals just want what we all want. To be loved!

PetFinder.com

The Virtual Home of Pet Adoption

PetFinder.com is the virtual home of 323,969 adoptable pets from 13,841 adoption groups. PetFinder.com offers a wide assortment of valuable opportunities to deliver your message to an active, qualified audience of individuals and families looking to adopt a pet. PetFinder.com is an on-line searchable database of animals who need homes. It is also a directory of more than 13,000 animal shelters and adoption organizations across the U.S., Canada and Mexico. Organizations maintain their own home pages and available pet databases. PetFinder's mission is to use internet technology and the resources it can generate to:

Increase public awareness of the availability of high-quality adoptable pets, increase the overall effectiveness of pet adoption programs across North America to the extent that the euthanasia of adoptable pets is eliminated, and elevate the status of pets to that of family member. From the comfort of their personal computers, pet lovers can search for a pet that best matches their needs. They can then reference a shelter's web page and discover what services it offers. PetFinder.com also includes classified ads, discussion forums and a library of animal welfare articles. From banners to sponsorships, promotions to integrated content, PetFinder.com will work with you to create the most compelling program for your specific marketing needs. Advertising opportunities are available. Go to www.petfinder.com to find Your forever Friend!

PetFinder.com is the virtual home
of 323,969 adoptable pets from
13,841 adoption groups.

Part Seven

◆

A Poem...

Written to Honor
All Homeless and Abused Animals
and Those Who Help Them!

Please Help Control the Pet Overpopulation.
Have Your Pet Spayed or Neutered!

A Different Kind of Homeless!

Look into my eyes and you will see
I'm just like you—wanting to be loved.
Just give me a chance to show you
How wonderful life will be by adopting me!

I come in all shapes, sizes and any breed,
Rescuing me, will be a life-long good deed.

Look into my eyes and you will see
I'm just like you—wanting to be loved.
Just give me a chance to show you
How wonderful life will be by adopting me!

I bark, I meow, I tweet, I may even have a shell,
When rescuing me, a "tale" for sure you will have to tell.

Look into my eyes and you will see
I'm just like you—wanting to be loved.
Just give me a chance to show you
How wonderful life will be by adopting me!

I may have been starved, or abused,
I may have been hit, or for bad purposes used.

Look into my eyes and you will see
I'm just like you—wanting to be loved.
Just give me a chance to show you
How wonderful life will be by adopting me!

I may be a puppy, a kitten, a dog or a cat,
Just put your hand on my little head and give me a pat.

Look into my eyes and you will see
I'm just like you—wanting to be loved.
Just give me a chance to show you
How wonderful life will be by adopting me!

Young or old, big or little, any color, feathered, finned or furry,
Don't hesitate, it may be too late, so please, oh please do hurry!

Look into my eyes and you will see
I'm just like you—wanting to be loved.
Just give me a chance to show you
How wonderful life will be by adopting me!

I am any time, any place, in a box or paper bag,
Sometimes I'm thrown away just like an old rag.

Look into my eyes and you will see

I'm just like you—wanting to be loved.

Just give me a chance to show you

How wonderful life will be by adopting me!

In the woods, a dumpster, shelter, yard or barn, you'll hear me cry,

Not always seen, so look hard because I am always nearby.

Look into my eyes and you will see

I'm just like you—wanting to be loved.

Just give me a chance to show you

How wonderful life will be by adopting me!

In warm, sunny weather or frigid cold and snow

It's me! I'm here! That is what I want YOU to know!

Look into my eyes and you will see

I'm just like you—wanting to be loved.

Just give me a chance to show you

How wonderful life will be by adopting me!

So be brave, be my hero, rescue me, adopt me

You and I, forever friends, we will be.

Look into my eyes and you will see

I'm just like you—wanting to be loved.

Just give me a chance to show you

How wonderful life will be by adopting me!

So Please Remember,

There is Always Room in the Inn. . .

For Me, A DIFFERENT KIND OF HOMELESS!

About the Author

The author with Sami Two

Ashleigh Rose Bottorff has been a pet owner since childhood, including dogs, cats, rabbits, a horse, two ponies and five ducks. Being a Midwestern farmer's daughter, as a young child she was given a horse, but only if she promised to muck out the stall, with no help, including in Midwestern winters. She promised and that's where it all started and as they say, "the rest is history". She went on to own many, many animals and to this day, lives in a rescued "zoo". Seeing animals in distress, getting phone calls from as far away as 200 miles about a kitten dumped in a cornfield, stopping traffic in busy intersections to help an animal in harm's way, missing a morning of college classes to "de-skunk" a stray dog, or just coming home to yet another "mystery" animal left on her door step, this author's life is never boring. She has worked for two veterinarians and the local animal shelter, checks boxes on the side of the road for dumped animals and lives for her passion of raising awareness of the importance of spay/neuter. She has written an article on pet travel. To feed her rescued "zoo", the author has been a self-employed marketing consultant for over 35 years that includes writing, job coaching and sales. The author, being a major caretaker has volunteered at her local hospital emergency room and physical therapy department, worked with seniors at luncheons and in adult foster care homes, tutored English, reading and writing, volunteered at her local elementary school, been the loudest "cheerleader" at kids' sports games and continues to rescue critters and strives to make the world a better place for everyone. Her motto for life is simple: "Kids and critters make the world go 'round. Live, love, hug and pray!"